99p

YORK NOTES

General Editors: Professor A.N. Jeffares (*University of Stirling*) & Professor Suheil Bushrui (*American University of Beirut*)

Harold Pinter

THE CARETAKER

Notes by G.M. Stephen

BA (LEEDS) PH D (SHEFFIELD)
Teacher of English, Haileybury College

GW00467609

LONGMAN
YORK PRESS

Extracts from *The Caretaker* by Harold Pinter are reprinted by kind permission
of Eyre Methuen Ltd, London, and Grove Press Inc., New York.
© 1960 by Theatre Promotions Ltd.

YORK PRESS
Immeuble Esseily, Place Riad Solh, Beirut.

LONGMAN GROUP LIMITED
Burnt Mill,
Harlow, Essex

© Librairie du Liban 1981

First published 1981
ISBN 0 582 78155 8

Printed in Hong Kong by
Wing Tai Cheung Printing Co. Ltd.,

Contents

Part 1

Introduction

The life of Harold Pinter

Harold Pinter was born on 10 October 1930 in Hackney, a working-class suburb in East London. His parents were Jewish, of either Hungarian or Portuguese stock. Hyman (Jack) Pinter was a ladies' tailor, hard-working and mildly prosperous, and Harold was to be his only child. Harold spent his first nine years living in the East End of London, much of it at a house in Thistlewaite Road, near to Clapton Pond. Early interviews given by Pinter draw a bleak picture of conditions in his childhood, and suggest a world of filthy canals, decaying housing, and factories belching smoke. In later years, Pinter has corrected this description, stating that he lived quite pleasantly in a comfortable terraced house. Pinter's home may have been quite comfortable (his mother was an excellent cook, and though his father had to work twelve hours a day, he brought home a reasonable income); but life could not always have been easy for a Jewish boy in London's East End in the 1930s. The area was a racial melting-pot: apart from native-born Londoners, there was a large Jewish community, many of whom had come to London in the early years of the twentieth century in order to escape persecution in Europe, particularly in Russia.

The First World War (1914–18) added a further flood of refugees, and by the time Pinter was born there were sizeable Chinese, Irish, and Negro communities in the East End. The 1930s were a time of economic depression, and this in turn led to political and racial unrest, perhaps almost inevitably in so mixed a community. In particular, the growing Fascist movement posed a threat to the Jewish community, and the period saw continual violent contact between the Fascists and their two main enemies, the Jews and the Communists.

This conflict did not die out with the Second World War (1939–45), and in very recent times London's East End has been in the newspaper headlines as a centre of racial conflict. Pinter could hardly have been unaware of this conflict in his youth, and it may even be responsible for the atmosphere of brooding menace that features in so many of his plays; but equally well its significance in his early life must not be overestimated. He was involved in fights, and surrounded by an atmosphere of suppressed violence, but his home was stable and happy.

Disruption came in 1939. In common with thousands of London children, Pinter was evacuated to the country when war broke out between Great Britain and Germany, to avoid the feared effects of German bombing. He was first evacuated to a 'castle in Cornwall', and then to somewhere nearer London, returning home in 1944 just as the first of the 'flying bombs' began to descend on London. Pinter described himself at this time as 'quite a morose little boy', and recorded that when the family had to evacuate the house during raids, the first thing he took with him was a cricket bat. Cricket, and sport in general, have been lasting interests of Pinter's. He was educated at Hackney Downs Grammar School, and whilst there played an active part in cricket and soccer, establishing a school record in running events. He left school in 1947, but not before one of his teachers, Joseph Brearley, had inspired in him a fierce love of drama.

At that time a knowledge of Latin was required of candidates wishing to enter most British universities, and Pinter had no Latin. Instead, he managed to obtain a grant to study at RADA, the world-famous Royal Academy of Dramatic Art in London. At the time it must have seemed a brave, and even foolhardy, decision. Although he had acted at school, he had seen little professional theatre, and appears to have known very little about it. His decision to act may have seemed even more ill-advised when he found himself unhappy at RADA (it has been suggested that he found the other students too sophisticated), and left after two terms. In order to do this, he faked a nervous breakdown, and for some time at least continued to draw his grant, and keep his parents ignorant of what had happened.

In 1948, when he was eighteen, he received his call-up for national service. This was the system that used to operate in Britain whereby all young men had to serve two years in the armed forces. Pinter declared himself a conscientious objector: someone whose moral beliefs compel him to denounce war and refuse to engage in military service. This decision could have resulted in a jail sentence, but fortunately for him he received only a fine.

In 1950, two major events in his life took place. Both were in one sense relatively minor, but they did mark the path his life was to take. He had two poems printed in a magazine called *Poetry London*, and he undertook his first professional engagement as an actor, speaking in a radio programme entitled *Focus on Football Pools*. However, rather more glamorous engagements were to follow. In 1951 he gained a part in a radio production of Shakespeare's *Henry VIII*, and resumed his training as an actor at London's Central School of Speech and Drama. In September 1951 he joined a company of actors who were touring plays around Ireland, spending nearly a year with them. Then, in 1953, he achieved another breakthrough. He was selected to appear in a season of classic plays being mounted at the King's Theatre, Hammersmith, London, by Sir Donald Wolfit (1902-68), a famous actor and theatre manager. It was here that he first met Vivien Merchant, an actress. They were to be married in 1956.

Between 1954 and 1957 Pinter was acting regularly in various provincial repertory companies. Up to this point in his life there had been little remarkable about his career; he seemed established as a moderately successful actor, and as a minor poet. All this changed in 1957. Rather tentatively, Pinter offered to write a play for a friend who was studying in the drama department of the University of Bristol. Pressed to produce something, Pinter wrote *The Room* in four days, squeezing his writing into the afternoons when he was rehearsing one play in the morning and performing in another in the evening. The play was produced by the drama department, went well, and was also produced by the drama school attached to the Old Vic Theatre in Bristol. This latter production was entered for a student drama festival held annually and sponsored by the newspaper *The Sunday Times*. There it attracted the attention of Harold Hobson, the influential drama critic of *The Sunday Times*. Soon a London theatre manager and impresario asked Pinter for any other plays he had written, and Pinter submitted *The Dumb Waiter* and *The Birthday Party*, the latter originally being entitled *The Party*.

The Birthday Party was accepted, and first performed at the Arts Theatre, Cambridge, England, on 28 April 1958. On 19 May it opened in London, at the Lyric Theatre. It was a disaster. It ran for only six nights before being taken off, and was almost universally condemned by the critics. They complained that it was 'just not funny enough', and almost totally obscure. One lone voice came out in defence of Pinter. Harold Hobson, the drama critic who had first spotted him, announced that he 'possesses the most original, disturbing and arresting talent in theatrical London.' He described *The Birthday Party* as 'absorbing', 'witty', and 'fascinating', and isolated one of the play's most marked features, an atmosphere of 'delicious, impalpable and hair-raising terror'. However, Hobson's was very much a lone voice, as it had been when he hailed Samuel Beckett's play *Waiting for Godot* (first performed in France in 1953) as a masterpiece of twentieth-century drama.

Pinter could hardly have foreseen at this time that in a mere eight years he would be receiving the title of Commander of the Order of the British Empire (CBE) in a list of honours awarded by the Queen of England, an award that marked his status as the leading British dramatist of the time. As it was, it did not take long for *The Birthday Party* to be accepted as a major play by a major playwright. In 1959 it was performed by a semi-amateur company, the Tavistock Players, in London; the production was excellent, and the play received some favourable reviews. It was also performed in Germany in the same year, and in the United States in 1960. In 1964 the play was revived at one of

London's most famous theatres, the Aldwych; and in 1968 a film of it was made. It had already been televised in 1960.

After *The Birthday Party* Pinter wrote various plays, among them *The Dumb Waiter* and *A Slight Ache*, a radio play broadcast in July 1959; but the real breakthrough came in April 1960, when *The Caretaker* opened at London's Arts Theatre Club. It was well received by the critics, one of whom even went so far as to describe it as 'a fine play'. It was *The Caretaker* that established Pinter's reputation, and after its first run in London it followed what was almost becoming a standard pattern for Pinter's work. It was performed in several countries, most notably in Germany, France, and the United States. Rather surprisingly the play was welcomed, as *The Birthday Party* had been, by Noel Coward (1899–1973), a famous author of elegant high comedy, and a staunch upholder of the British theatrical tradition. In 1962 Coward joined with a number of other famous theatrical personalities, including the film star Richard Burton (b.1925), to finance the making of a film of *The Caretaker*. The film was to win major prizes at the Berlin Film Festival of 1963.

Pinter has never ceased to be an active writer, and the years that followed *The Caretaker* have been extremely busy ones for him. His best known full-length plays have been *The Homecoming* (1965), *Old Times* (1971), *No Man's Land* (1975), and *Betrayal* (1978). He has written and appeared in plays for television, and been responsible for a number of film scripts, amongst them *The Servant* (1962), *The Pumpkin Eater* (1965), and *The Quiller Memorandum* (1966). In 1973 he was appointed an Associate Director of the National Theatre in London.

Harold Pinter's life can be seen as falling into two sections, the first lasting until 1957, the period when he was a successful actor with the stage name of David Baron. After 1957, although he continued to act, the main centre of interest became his work as a dramatist. This latter has been extremely diverse, and has spread into a wide range of areas, notably the live theatre, television, radio, and film. He has now reached a position where he is acknowledged, at least by some critics, as Britain's greatest living playwright.

The work of Harold Pinter

Despite his work as a poet, an actor, a director, and a writer for films, Pinter's reputation rests squarely on his full-length plays. The best known of these are probably *The Birthday Party*, *The Caretaker*, *The Homecoming*, *No Man's Land*, and *Betrayal*. There are many others that could reasonably claim a place in any list of his most outstanding work. The wise student will draw up his own list, on the basis of as wide a reading as possible of Pinter's work.

It is fashionable to talk of Pinter's work in terms of 'comedies of menace' and 'social comedies'. This division can be misleading. It has arisen because of what can appear to be quite a marked division between an early play, such as *The Birthday Party*, and a later one such as *No Man's Land*. In the early plays, the audience are made to laugh, but at the same time are threatened by a violent, hostile presence that often destroys one or more of the central characters. In the later plays there is less violence, rather more subtle comic effects, and much less obscurity. However, the critic's urge to categorise an author's work and place it in neatly-separated compartments is not a healthy one, at least when applied to Pinter's work, which evolves rather than changes; and certain concerns (loneliness, failure and personal inadequacy, communication, menace, the place of the artist in society, personal identity) are never absent from his plays. As he has become older Pinter has relied less on gimmicks and melodramatic stage effects, told his audiences more about his characters, and made his plays more naturalistic. In physical, outward terms, less happens in a later Pinter play, but the difference is merely one of emphasis: just as much is happening inside the minds of his characters.

Pinter has been hailed by many critics as Britain's 'greatest living playwright', and has received more critical attention than perhaps any modern British dramatist. In itself this does not mean very much; a number of authors have been hailed as geniuses by their own generations, and discarded by the next. Nor does it really matter whether he is the greatest living British dramatist, or merely one of the contenders for the title: history, not present-day critics, will show how he should finally be rated. What is true is that he has been a major influence on modern British drama, and something of a revolutionary. Unlike many revolutionaries, he has managed to keep on surprising his audiences and critics after his first breakthrough, and he cannot be described as anything other than a major figure in twentieth-century drama.

The literary and historical background

Pinter's life spans three distinct periods in British history: the period prior to the outbreak of the Second World War in 1939, the post-war period, and the time from the mid-1960s to the present day. Vast changes have occurred during this time, including severe economic depression, a world war, the loss of Britain's empire, and a continuing process whereby the country has sought to come to terms with its new status in the world, and allied itself to Europe. Dramatists are not simply social historians, and Pinter has firmly resisted any attempts to interpret his plays on a purely political or social level. Nevertheless, an author cannot help being influenced to a certain extent by the age in which he lives. This can occur on a superficial level, as when an author uses slang or collo-quial language that is firmly linked to one particular society or time; and on a deeper level when an author chooses to examine in his work subjects or ideas that are a particular concern of the age in which he lives. Thus Shakespeare is very concerned in many of his plays with the role and nature of kingship, naturally enough in an age when the well-being of every person in a country could depend on the efficiency with which a monarch did his job. Great authors have tended to write on subjects which, though they might be concerns of their own age, also have a universal significance. Thus whilst Shakespeare wrote for his contemporaries on the subject of kingship, modern audiences can see in his work wide-ranging comment on the whole nature of good govern-ment, a subject which is relevant to every age and generation. This forms one reason why so few critics are willing to commit themselves, to say that an author such as Pinter will continue to be admired and hailed as a great playwright in the future. He is undoubtedly admired today, but it is often very difficult for people who are themselves a pro-duct of the same age as the author to see whether what he is writing about is of purely topical interest, or whether it will have a lasting significance for theatre audiences.

Mention has already been made of the possible influence of the 1930s on Pinter's writing, in terms of suppressed violence and a sense of menace. The Second World War may well have been an equal influ-ence. Britain occupied an almost unique position in this conflict. It was not invaded, as were France and many other European countries; nor was it left unmarked by direct conflict, as were the United States and many Commonwealth countries. Instead it was under constant threat of invasion, and continually brought face to face with the realities of conflict by incessant bombing raids. It is not difficult to see the par-ticular atmosphere of these times pervading Pinter's plays, especially the early ones. In particular the hidden menace and sudden eruptions of violence that are a feature of Pinter's early plays could almost act as an emblem for the state of mind of many Londoners in the 1940s, when air raids could come at any time, people lived constantly under threat, and a few seconds could turn what had been a home into a bomb-blasted ruin. Here, as in Pinter's plays, the enemy was faceless, hostile, and always waiting to pounce. Pinter himself was evacuated and had to leave his home in the war, and the sense of rootlessness, loneliness, and isola-tion that can be seen in a character such as Davies in *The Caretaker* may have its origin in Pinter's own experience as an evacuee. However, it is always dangerous to push the links between an author's work and his life too far, and any suggestion that Pinter's plays are an attempt to study or evoke the mood of any one particular time should be dis-missed. Whatever his plays are, they are much wider in scope than that.

Pinter is often linked with the so-called 'New Wave' of British dramatists who came to prominence after 1956. There is no doubt that in the mid-1950s British drama, which had been relatively stagnant and backward-looking for a number of years, was revitalised by the appearance of several new young dramatists, with perhaps the most notable being John Osborne (b.1929), Arnold Wesker (b.1932), and John Arden (b.1930). Osborne's *Look Back in Anger* (1956) was the play which spearheaded this revolution. It had as its central figure Jimmy Porter, the 'angry young man' oppressed by a stagnant and out-moded society, and contained a stimulating mixture of invective and social criticism. Many of the New Wave dramatists began their work with the English Stage Company, playing at the Royal Court Theatre in London, and had in common their age, a socialist outlook, and a flair for experimental drama.

It is easy to see how it is that Pinter has come to be linked with these dramatists. He was born at roughly the same time as many of them, he came from a working-class background, and started to write plays in the mid-1950s. Some of his plays were presented at the Royal Court, under the auspices of the English Stage Company, and much of his work was clearly experimental. However, a glance at some of the major plays of the New Wave dramatists, such as Wesker's *Chicken Soup with Barley* (1958) and *Chips with Everything* (1962), and Arden's *Serjeant Musgrave's Dance* (1959), shows how wide the gap is that exists between them and Pinter. Their work is often directly political, rebellious, and a complaint against a class-ridden and hollow society. Much of this is lost on Pinter; he is rarely political in his plays, hardly concerned about class except indirectly, and writes about individuals rather than society as a whole. Indeed, the individual differences between the New Wave authors are so marked as to render the term suspect as a useful definition, and whilst the student of Pinter should read *Look Back in Anger* for purposes of comparison, it is unlikely that the exercise will greatly increase his understanding of Pinter.

Much more relevant to Pinter is a study of Samuel Beckett's *Waiting for Godot*, and those plays which have been described as 'Drama of the Absurd'. This whole area can be a nightmare for the inexperienced student, largely because the authors supposedly involved in the movement are often very dissimilar, frequently highly obscure, and have caused some critics to write explanatory books more obscure than the works they were meant to clarify. Some of the more notable authors in this group are Edward Albee (b.1928), Samuel Beckett (b.1906), Jean Genet (b.1910), Eugene Ionesco (b.1912), and N.F. Simpson (b.1919). Many of these dramatists present their audiences with characters stripped of all non-essentials, such as decent clothes, employment, a routine of family life, in an attempt to reduce man to his basic nature, and ascertain what this is. Often the conclusion is that man is a hollow shell: when non-essentials are taken away, there is nothing left at all. People are seen to be filling their lives with routine, trivial things, so that they do not have to think about the essential hopelessness of their situation and the basic emptiness of their lives. Seen in this light, man's life is absurd because it is totally without purpose, or any aim except that of surviving the next day without coming face to face with the meaninglessness of existence. This theme need not necessarily be gloomy, as the dramatist's point is often that life is only meaningless because its basic nature is not understood. If humans could only face up to the fact that they were alone in the universe with no divine purpose to their lives, then a realistic mode of living could be thought out. However, it is true to say that most of the dramatists show their audience the meaninglessness of life, but give little idea of there being any hope for a new life.

Dramatists of the absurd believed that life was not rational; that it did not follow any laws or logical pattern. Where they were revolutionary was in the fact that they transferred this irrationality to the stage. Their plays often have no plot as such, make a nonsense of chronology, and contain obscure or unexplained incidents. Plays of this nature were a great shock to audiences when they were first performed. They obeyed none of the laws of conventional drama, and because absurdity is amusing, the plays were frequently very comic. Nor were these plays 'about' something, in the sense of having a specific moral or point to them. Instead, they were capable of widely differing interpretations. Beckett's *Waiting for Godot* has been seen as a play about religion, as a criticism of capitalism, and a play about German-occupied France in the Second World War, to name but a few views. The similarities between this style of drama and Pinter's plays such as *The Birthday Party* and *The Caretaker* are clear: the latter are comic, leave audiences confused about the origins of characters and the truth of what they say, show behaviour that can appear absurd and pointless, and are open to many different interpretations. The differences are also there, in that Pinter's plays are more tightly constructed, psychologically more probing, and outwardly closer to real life in what they portray. However, Pinter has admitted that Beckett was a major influence on his writing, and no student of Pinter can afford not to have read *Waiting for Godot*. If he does so, he may well feel that he is on ground that is at least partially familiar. To bring the student back to earth, it should be noted that Noel Coward, a totally conventional albeit very skilful author of elegant comedies, was also very much admired by Pinter. With all this discussion of other authors, it must also be firmly stated that the biggest influence on Pinter's writing is Pinter himself, and that no amount of background reading can compensate for a detailed study of what Pinter himself wrote.

A note on the text

There are no textual problems with Pinter's work. *The Caretaker* was first published in 1960; the revised, reset, and reprinted edition was published by Eyre Methuen, London, 1967. All Pinter's plays are published by Eyre Methuen, and include *The Birthday Party* (1959), *The Homecoming* (1965), and *No Man's Land* (1975). *Betrayal* was published in 1978. Methuen have also produced a very valuable three-volume collection of Pinter's plays up to 1969 (see Part 5). In the United States, Pinter's plays are published by Grove Press, New York.

Part 2

Summaries
of THE CARETAKER

A general summary

Mick, a young man, is sitting silently in a junk-filled room. When he hears the noise of Aston, his brother, and Davies, a tramp, entering the house, he leaves without meeting them. Aston makes Davies welcome, and, with Davies doing most of the talking, it emerges that Aston has rescued Davies from a fight in the café where he was working, caused by an argument over who was to empty a bucket of rubbish. Aston only uses the one room, but says he is 'in charge' of the whole house. Davies complains about his shoes, and describes his attempts to beg a new pair from a monastery: he refuses to wear the pair that Aston offers him. Davies is to spend the night in the room, and he tells Aston how he needs to get down to Sidcup to get his papers, which will prove his identity. In the morning, Aston tells Davies that he has been talking in his sleep.

When he leaves Davies starts to explore the room, but Mick enters and grabs Davies, forcing him to the floor. Mick suddenly becomes polite, and questions Davies, but refuses to give Davies his trousers. Mick says he owns the house, and treats Davies as someone who might be able to buy it. Aston enters with a bag that is supposedly the one Davies left at the café, and there is a short struggle for possession of the bag, which Davies eventually wins. Mick leaves, and Aston tells how Mick wants him to decorate the room and the house. He admits that the bag is not Davies's, but another one that he has been able to buy cheaply. Aston offers Davies the job of caretaker to the house. Later on, Davies enters the room in darkness, and is chased by Mick with a vacuum cleaner. A terrified Davies draws a knife, but Mick puts the light on and explains that he was merely doing some cleaning. Mick offers a sandwich to Davies, and confides in him that he is worried about his brother, who does not appear to like work. Mick then also offers Davies the job of caretaker, if Davies can produce his references from Sidcup. In the morning, Aston wakes up Davies, who has again been making a lot of noise in his sleep. Davies complains about an open window. Aston then talks about how he was taken away to a mental hospital, and operated on, since which time he has been unable to think clearly. Some time later, Davies is complaining to Mick about Aston, and Mick tells Davies about his dreams for the house, which will be decorated in the most modern style. Davies demands a clock. Aston offers Davies another pair of shoes, which are grudgingly accepted.

At night, Aston complains about the noise Davies is making, and Davies taunts him with his revelations about having been in a mental hospital and undergoing an operation. Aston demands that Davies leave the house, which he does unwillingly. Later he returns with Mick, who appears friendly, but suddenly insists that Davies had told him he was an experienced interior decorator. When Davies says that Aston is insane, Mick dismisses him and demands that he leave. Davies tries to plead with both brothers, but cannot get them to change their minds.

Detailed summaries

The Caretaker is written in three acts. For detailed study, it is necessary to split the play up into smaller sections or scenes, and these are identified by the page number on which each scene starts (based on the 1967 edition of the play published by Eyre Methuen), and the first few words of the scene. These scene divisions are made purely for critical convenience, and are not to be found in the text itself.

Act 1, Scene 1, page 7: 'Mick is alone in the room . . .'

Mick is sitting alone in a room that is full of old furniture and an assortment of odd items. He leaves silently when he hears Aston and Davies entering the house. Aston speaks only a few words, but makes Davies, a tramp, welcome in the room. Davies accepts some of Aston's tobacco for his pipe, and complains about conditions in the café in which he was working. He says he left his wife because he found her washing her underclothes in a saucepan used for cooking vegetables. It appears that Davies has had an argument with someone in the café over who should take a bucket of rubbish outside, and has been fired as a result. Aston has rescued him from what could have been a violent removal from the café. Davies complains that he has left his bag containing all his possessions at the café.

Davies asks about the house, and is upset when he hears that foreigners occupy some of its other rooms. He complains that he has no wearable shoes, and when Aston produces a pair, tells a long story about trying to beg a pair of shoes from a monastery, where a monk told him to 'piss off'. He refuses the shoes Aston has offered him. Aston offers Davies a bed, and says how he wants to build a shed in the garden behind the house. Davies asks about a statue of Buddha that is on the shelf, one of the many items Aston seems to have acquired, and then begs some money from Aston. He talks about how he must get down to Sidcup, to pick up his 'papers', as he has been living under the assumed name of

Bernard Jenkins, and needs documents to prove who he really is. He admits that he left these papers with someone in Sidcup nearly fifteen years ago. Davies climbs into bed. Aston is fiddling with a plug and a screwdriver.

COMMENTARY:

The silent exit of Mick from the room at the start of the play is mysterious and menacing, both of which elements feature largely in the particular atmosphere of almost any Pinter play. In thematic terms, the incident has little meaning or significance, but it points to a feature of Pinter's work that is often overlooked in the rush to decide what his plays mean. He is a superb dramatist, in the sense that he is extremely skilful in evoking atmosphere and manipulating the emotional response of his audiences. Thus Mick's presence on the stage, and his exit, create tension, interest, and excitement almost before the play has started. The stage directions before Act 1, and throughout the play, are very detailed and specific, more so than in earlier Pinter plays; by specifying exactly the objects in the room, and the appearance of the characters, Pinter may be trying to emphasise the reality of the play, and discourage directors from any attempt to render it as an abstract production. The characters each have a distinctive speech pattern: Davies is garrulous, rambling, and often speaks in fragmented phrases, whilst Aston is almost monosyllabic. Davies's racial prejudice becomes apparent almost immediately, as does his laziness, ill-temper, and bitterness. He can be seen as a portrait of the worst type of British worker, being quarrelsome and unwilling to do anything that requires the slightest bit of extra effort, such as taking the bucket out. There is considerable comedy in this opening scene, notably Davies's description of finding his wife's underwear in the vegetable pan, and his extremely unlikely assertion that a monk told him to 'piss off'. There is also the sequence where Davies praises at great length shoes made of leather, appears delighted with the shoes that Aston has found for him, and then after a pause announces 'Don't fit though', thus dismissing the shoes and providing the audience with a richly anti-climactic moment. As well as comedy, there is menace, a hint of violence, and uncertainty. The audience still have Mick in mind, do not yet know who or what Aston is, and are treated to a quite vivid description of the fight that Davies was nearly involved in.

There is little plot in *The Caretaker*, in the sense that the play is built round characters rather than events, and one danger that exists in writing a play constructed in this manner is that it will become formless, rambling, and lack continuity. To counter this danger, Pinter inserts several phrases, objects, and incidents into this first scene which reappear later: the statue of Buddha that Mick eventually smashes, Davies's lost bag, his sensitivity to draughts, the gas stove, his lack of shoes, Sidcup and his papers, the leak in the roof, and Davies's question 'What do you think I am, a wild animal?' These all appear later in the play, and thus give it a degree of unity and continuity that otherwise it might lack.

Perhaps the main feature of interest in this opening section is the broaching of some of the play's major concerns. Davies's proposed visit to Sidcup highlights and acts as a symbol for two of these, namely the crisis of identity, and people's dreams. Davies is a rambler, a vagrant with no roots, no home, and no base. He is a rootless person, lacking both self-knowledge and a sense of his own identity. In his own mind he believes that Sidcup and his papers will give him these things that he lacks, create him as an individual, and allow him to go out and face the world. The audience suspect that the journey will never take place (later in the play Davies seems not to want it to happen, perhaps because it is his last hope and actually going to Sidcup would shatter his comforting illusions); and that even if it does, papers left with someone fifteen years ago are unlikely to be still available. Davies and Sidcup are therefore symbols of rootless people, and of the manner in which humans fight their own sense of inadequacy and gain the strength to carry on living through the means of unrealistic dreams. Sidcup and his papers are hardly real any more to Davies, but the belief that he could one day go there gives a sense of purpose and hope to an otherwise completely aimless life. If Sidcup is Davies's dream, then building the shed at the back of the house is Aston's. It, too, is never likely to happen, but it gives Aston something to aim for in a pointless existence. In talking about the shed, Aston is convincing himself that he can produce something tangible, and do practical things. Like Davies and Sidcup, the shed is tied to Aston's sense of personal identity, and is the magic formula that will start his life off on a new track.

Communication is another concern that is very apparent in this first section. Davies and Aston are clearly trying to communicate in their speech with each other. Pinter has said that speech is often an attempt to evade true communication, that people hide behind words, and that what a person does not say is often more revealing than what he does say. Both these suggestions are evident in Davies's words. His aggressiveness and his boasting ('I've had dinner with the best') are an attempt to boost the feeble and inadequate person that he really is. Davies's speeches are meant to impress Aston: what they actually do is reveal him as he really is, and show the battle that is taking place inside his head between pride and a desperate need for shelter and a bed. Aston also talks, but it is his actions not his words that reveal his kindness and need for friendship (his giving tobacco and money to Davies are two examples). Here, as in the rest of the play, words cannot bridge the gap between people, and the only person who listens closely to what is being said is the speaker himself.

NOTES AND GLOSSARY:

vest: an undergarment, not a waistcoat

treating me like dirt: treating me badly, as if I were an inferior person

When he come at me: When he looked as if he were going to attack me

loosen myself up: relax, calm down

done in: killed, murdered

a while: a short time

knocked off: stolen

Great West Road: the main road leading from London to the south-west of the British Isles

have a go: make an attack

skate: a skate is a large flat fish. In this context, it is used as a term of abuse

I've had dinner with the best: I have taken meals with upper-class people. This is certainly not true

toe-rags: literally, a piece of cloth used for wiping toes: another term of abuse

on the road: a vagrant or tramp

I keep myself up: I keep myself fit

handy: fit, a good fighter

I've had a few attacks: this means attacks of illness, not that Davies has been attacked by other people

parks: thrusts, pushes

git: fool, idiot; a colloquial term of abuse

standing: status

You got an eye of him, did you?: You saw what he looked like, did you?

the guvnor give me the bullet: the manager fired me, dismissed me from my job

he'd have landed: he had managed to hit me

bob: colloquial term for one shilling, now worth five new pence

kipping: sleeping

landing: an upstairs corridor or passage with rooms leading off it

Get away: You don't say! Colloquial phrase implying mock amazement and disbelief

doing to: repair

caff: café, small restaurant

knick-knacks: odds and ends, assorted trivial items

Luton: a town in southern England, north of London

Shepherd's Bush: an area in central London

convenience:	a public toilet or lavatory
Acton:	a suburb of London
Not bad trim:	not in a bad state of repair
Piss off:	to piss is offensive slang, meaning to urinate. In this context, it means go away
a bite:	any food
en I?:	haven't I?
ate it:	eaten it
mother superior:	monks are people who take vows of chastity, poverty, and obedience to the teachings of Christianity, and to carry out these vows live in monasteries in a community with other monks. Women who take the same vows are called nuns, and live in nunneries or convents. It is a monastery that Davies calls at in Luton, and so it would have an abbot at its head; a mother superior is the woman in charge of a group of nuns, and it would be extremely rude to suggest to a monk, as Davies does, that he was ruled by a mother superior
hooligan:	a vandal, or disreputable and badly-behaved young person
cleared out:	went away rapidly
Watford:	a large town a few miles north-west of London
North Circular:	a ring road that circles the north of London
Hendon:	an area in the north-west of London
flog:	sell
Not much cop:	not worth very much, not much use
look out:	find
the weather to break:	the weather to improve
do it?:	does it?
en't they?:	aren't they?
Guinness:	a very popular Irish stout, black in colour, now brewed in England as well as Dublin
Sidcup:	a medium-sized town fourteen miles south of London
insurance card:	anyone who works in the British Isles is required to pay National Insurance, a system whereby in return for weekly or monthly payments the government guarantees unemployment pay, a basic pension, and other benefits. Proof of payment is by stamps that are stuck on to a card
in the nick:	in jail
nigs:	niggers. Used here as a term of abuse
the war:	presumably the Second World War (1939–45)

about near on: nearly
done in: tired, worn out

Scene 2, page 21: 'Lights up. Morning.'

It is the next morning, and Aston tells Davies that Davies has been making a noise during the night, groaning and jabbering. Davies strenuously denies this, and blames the coloured people sleeping in the other rooms. Aston is going out to buy a saw, and Davies is surprised that he is considered trustworthy enough to be left alone in the room. Before he goes out, Aston tells Davies how a woman made a sexual proposition to him in a café; and Davies says he might go out himself later to try and find another job in a café. When Aston leaves, Davies searches through all the many different items that are in the room. Mick enters silently when Davies is rummaging through a drawer, and attacks him, pinning him to the floor. Eventually he sits down, with Davies still on the floor, and asks him a single question, about what he is doing in the room.

COMMENTARY:
The basis of future conflict between Aston and Davies can already be seen in the polite complaints that Aston makes about Davies's noisy sleeping, and Davies's aggressive denial of the accusation. Davies, of course, blames 'them Blacks', thus showing how race hatred is often only the result of people wishing their own failings on to someone else, and thus absolving themselves of guilt. Aston's trust of Davies reveals his essentially kindly nature, but the story about the woman offering to let him look at her body seems clumsy. It can be explained as indicative of the way a mentally-retarded person's mind jumps from one topic to another (although Aston rarely does this elsewhere in the play), an aspect of Pinter's distrust of women, or as a device to keep the audience confused and uncertain. The story has a shock effect, but it can be argued that it is too obvious a technique, and is out of place and pointless. Aston's questioning of Davies about his name and where he came from makes Davies nervous, and emphasises his rootlessness and lack of any fixed place in society.

There is further comedy in this scene, although it is tinged with something rather less than funny, namely a strong sense of Davies's inadequacies and boastfulness: he claims to have had offers from women similar to those Aston has had (most unlikely); and reveals comic but pathetic ignorance when he assumes that gas can leak from an unconnected gas cooker. This ignorance of ordinary domestic detail crops up again when Davies stresses how familiar he is with beds and sleeping in them, which only serves to remind the audience of how unfamiliar he is with the most basic item of furniture. A fact unremarked on by most critics is that the short period when Davies is alone in the room is one of the most touching in the whole play. In many ways, Davies is not an attractive figure, but the audience are aware that for the first time in many years he has been trusted, and he seems to be responding to this trust as he wanders happily around the room, exploring with a placid contentment and curiosity. He is behaving in a blameless and perfectly innocent manner when he is suddenly attacked and hurled to the floor by Mick. This sudden outbreak of violence in a hitherto placid atmosphere is a typical Pinter effect: the safe haven of the room is smashed by an eruption of raw violence and hostility that manages to suggest a malevolent outside world existing just out of sight of the audience. It is also a climactic ending to the first act, injecting a full measure of tension and suspense into the play.

NOTES AND GLOSSARY:

Dead out:	in a deep sleep
bloke:	person
Blacks:	an offensive slang term for Negroes and other people with dark skin
jig saw:	a mechanical saw used by carpenters and craftsmen
fret saw:	a small hand-held saw used where precise lines or intricate patterns have to be cut out of wood
Get out of it:	colloquial expression of amazement
couple of bob:	two shillings, or ten new pence
take any liberties:	take advantage of the situation
Wembley:	a suburb in north London
a bit of:	some
near on:	nearly
under way:	arranged, organised
sideboard:	a large piece of furniture with drawers, a flat surface, and shelving for plates and crockery in it
What's the game?:	What are you doing?

Act 2, Scene 3, page 30: 'A few seconds later.'

Mick changes suddenly from violent attacker into polite questioner, saying to Davies 'It's awfully nice to meet you.' In two long speeches Mick suggests a whole gallery of people he is reminded of by Davies, before, with another quick change of mood, he begins to interrogate Davies again in short, angry questions. Mick refuses to let Davies have his trousers, accuses him of lying when he tries to explain why he is in the room, and announces that he owns the house. He then threatens to take Davies to the police station in his van, but is soon apparently offering Davies the chance to buy the house. Aston enters, and Mick changes mood again, talking to Aston, his brother, about the leak in the roof of the house. Aston brings a bag for Davies, but Mick grabs it, hides it, and threatens Davies. The bag is then passed round from person to person until Davies manages to get it. He retreats to the bed, and tells Aston that he did not go out to Wembley as he had said he would.

COMMENTARY:

This scene centres around Mick. He is shown as a character who is prone to sudden changes of mood, from the oppressively polite to the cruelly overbearing and accusatory, and someone whose response can never be accurately predicted, least of all by Davies. His meeting with Davies shows a situation that is common in Pinter's plays, where two characters appear to be merely talking, but are in fact engaged in a battle for dominance and mastery over the other person. Some critics have seen in this a complex allegorical statement about the need of human beings to establish territorial rights over an area they claim as their own, and see in Mick's behaviour the workings of a primitive instinct to hurl out the intruder from one's own territory. Mick seems to be in love with words, and when he starts on a train of thought, he carries it on to ludicrous lengths until it is exhausted. Thus the mention of his brother's uncle leads on to a lengthy description of this man and his essentially incredible character and actions, which soon loses any relevance to the situation in hand. Similarly, a reference to 'a bloke I once knew in Shoreditch' is expanded into a tour of fifteen different areas or places in London, and detail is piled on detail until they all become meaningless. This is comic, but also unsettling.

Davies is a character in search of his identity, and Mick's list of people whom Davies resembles, and almost random catalogue of London suburbs, confuses Davies even more, and emphasises his rootlessness. The third time that Mick states Davies 'remind[s] me of a bloke . . .' Davies has to cut him off in anguish, in an attempt to stop this flow of recollections and establish his real self in it. The last section of Mick's long speech on pages 35–6 produces another list, this time of legal and technical terms; it is immensely cruel. In his previous lines, Mick has taunted Davies by appearing to think he could buy the house, when clearly he is in no position to do so. Mick's apparent assumption that Davies has enough money to do so only serves to emphasise Davies's poverty, in both financial and mental terms. This is cruel enough, but the concluding lines go one stage further. Mick produces a list of what society demands from its members when they are established as money-earners and family men ('down payments, back payments, family allowances, bonus schemes'). This is not only totally incomprehensible to Davies, but also a direct attack on one of his weakest points. He is a man whose life is dominated by his lost papers in Sidcup, and who has shown an irrational and deep-seated fear of the paperwork and form-filling that modern life demands, and it is this very aspect of life with which Mick bombards him. Perhaps Mick himself understands the terms he uses, perhaps not; it does not matter. Davies is so frightened of the legalities and technicalities of life that he responds with panic, and cannot question Mick's confident authority. The speech is funny because it is incongruous; it is ludicrous to think of Davies buying a house, or having a 'personal medical attendant'. But it is more than this. The legal, financial, and technical terms that Mick uses represent something that Davies has never understood, and because he has never understood them, he has come to fear them. It could be argued that it is this fear and the sense of inadequacy it has produced that have made Davies leave his papers behind in Sidcup and become a rootless vagrant, an outcast from society. He has been driven out by his inability to understand the technicalities of modern living, but Mick refuses him his escape, and brings him face to face with what he has been running away from. On a more minor level, it may be that Pinter is taking the opportunity to criticise modern jargon, as used in legal and financial dealings.

There are other features of some significance in this scene. The opening is something of a shock. It is normal for there to be an interval after Act 1 in most productions of *The Caretaker*, and the conventional way to start Act 2 would be after a lapse of time between the state of affairs in the play at the end of the first act and the start of the second. Instead Pinter picks up the action exactly where he had left it at the end of Act 1, ignoring the fact that the audience have probably been away from the play for twelve or fifteen minutes.

The incident where Davies's bag is passed around, hidden, kept from Davies, and finally restored to him is funny, but also symbolic. It is the sort of crude, physical humour that one might expect to find in an early film, but it has serious undertones. It reveals the conflicts and tensions that exist between the three characters, and also reveals them as what they are. Mick is the aggressor, the prime mover in keeping the bag from Davies, and his behaviour shows clearly how he enjoys taunting Davies. His sudden changes of mood and unpredictability are shown too, by the fact that it is he who eventually restores the bag to Davies, a contradiction of all his previous actions. Aston shows his generosity in trying to restore the bag to Davies, but shows also how much he is influenced by Mick: at one point, Aston gives the bag to Mick, perhaps hoping he will restore it to Davies. Davies is seen as the eternal victim, struggling to get his 'rights' from other people, and failing. His acquisitiveness and grasping nature are shown by the manner in which he clutches the bag to himself, and retreats fearfully to the bed.

Humour and violence are clearly present in the scene, as are various references to family. Logically, the 'uncle's brother' that Mick says Davies reminds him of must be Mick's father, and thus Mick seems to be saying that Davies reminds him of his father. Mick also refers to his mother's bed, and implies that Davies is insulting his mother. Some critics have seen the family as one of Pinter's major concerns in *The Caretaker*, but the references in this scene are hardly sufficient evidence to justify this argument. The main function of this scene must be the revelation of the conflict that exists between these three characters, and it does provide some evidence for the view that Mick sees Davies as a threat to his relationship with his brother, and so feels that he has to get rid of him. Davies, the outcast from society, seems destined to be cast out of the society in miniature that is represented by Aston, Mick, and the house.

NOTES AND GLOSSARY:

penchant:	(*French*) a leaning, fondness, or inclination for
Salvation Army:	founded in 1878 by William Booth (1829–1912), this was a religious and missionary body organised in a semi-military way to 'fight for Christ' and assist the poor and underprivileged. It is still in existence
Beckenham Reserves:	Mick is saying that his uncle's brother once played for the reserve team of a minor football club
fiddle:	violin
papoose:	a child of a Red (American) Indian family
Your spitting image he was:	he looked very like you, bore a striking physical resemblance
ain't:	is not
Shoreditch ... Dalston Junction:	the fifteen suburbs, streets, and buildings mentioned by Mick in this speech all exist in London, and are situated in various positions just out from the central area of the city. None of them are particularly well known, and this seems to be the only link between them
dead spit:	shortened form of 'spitting image'
arse:	offensive slang term meaning rectum or posterior
Guildford:	A large town to the south-west of London
by-pass:	a road that circles a city or town, thus diverting traffic away from the centre
Fibber:	liar. The term is normally used of someone who tells minor, insignificant lies
punch up:	fight
perky:	cheeky, insolent, impudent
mum:	mother

seven quid: seven pounds

Rateable value: Rates are a form of local taxation that operates throughout Great Britain. All owners of houses or property pay a certain amount each year towards the provision of water and power supplies, and other local services, the amount paid being decided on the basis of a 'rateable value' given to their property

keen: interested, eager

loitering with intent: in English law a person can be charged with the crime of loitering with intent to commit a crime

daylight robbery: a colloquial term not recognised in law, meaning to rob someone brazenly or openly, to make no secret of stealing from them. The term might be used when someone thinks they are being overcharged by a shopkeeper, or for some service they require

filching: stealing, robbing

West Ham: a working-class suburb of London

No strings attached: no conditions or further stipulations attached to the agreement

open and above board: legal, honest

down payments: when an article is to be purchased by a number of weekly, monthly, or yearly instalments, it is usually a requirement that the purchaser will provide a 'down payment' consisting of an agreed amount of the total purchase cost

back payments: payment of money that is owing, or which should have been paid earlier

family allowances: originally an allowance against income tax for a married man, or a man with children to support. These still exist, but nowadays the money is paid directly to the wife or mother

remission of term for good behaviour: the amount a prisoner can have his sentence reduced for good behaviour whilst in jail

compensation . . . double check: terms commonly used in insurance policies on life or property, stating what is and what is not covered by the insurance policy

carry the can: bear or take the responsibility

Scrub it: forget it, stop it

Scene 4, page 39: 'Mick goes to the door and exits.'

Mick leaves the room without any explanation, and Aston says that Mick is his brother, is in the building trade, and owns a van. Aston is meant to be decorating the upper storey of the house for him, but says he will only be able to concentrate on this when he has built his shed. Davies realises that the bag Aston has brought him is not his own, and Aston admits that he could not find the original bag, but bought this one cheaply. It has two check shirts in it, and a smoking jacket. Davies rejects the shirts, but takes the jacket, and Aston offers him the job of caretaker in the house, complete with white overalls.

COMMENTARY:
Davies may be destitute, but he is also (in Mick's words) 'choosy'. He refuses Aston's offer of shoes, and although he has no shirt at all, rejects the two check shirts that are in the bag, saying that he wants shirts with stripes on, because they are warmer. It is, of course, ludicrous to judge the warmth of a shirt by its pattern; but the incident reveals the extent to which human behaviour is illogical and unreasonable, and governed by emotion more than by practicality. Equally irrational is Davies's fondness for the smoking jacket, a luxury item that is of little or no practical use; but it is a rich man's item of clothing, and Davies prefers this to the much more practical shirts. Similarly, Aston offers Davies the job of caretaker; Davies has no job and no prospects, and this offer seems to be ideal for him, but he quibbles over details, accepting the offer not as a privilege, but as a right, something over which he can afford to dictate terms. His fear of being 'found out' dominates the final sequence.

NOTES AND GLOSSARY:
feller:	fellow, person
en'he:	isn't he?
doing up:	decorating, repairing
knock up:	build, make
after you:	chasing or following you
have me in:	put me in jail

Scene 5, page 44: 'Then up to dim light through the window.'

Davies comes into the room in darkness, cannot work the light switch, lights a match, drops the box, and finds it has been kicked out of his reach by an unseen presence. When Davies draws a knife, the vacuum cleaner lights up and pursues a terrified Davies across the room. The light goes on, and Mick explains that it was his turn to clean the room, and he was doing it in darkness because the only power available for the cleaner was from the light socket. Mick is friendly towards Davies, compliments him on the forceful speech he has just made, and offers him a sandwich. Mick confides in Davies that he is worried about Aston, whom he thinks does not like work, but when Davies seeks to take advantage of this, and says that he finds Aston 'a bit of a funny bloke', Mick turns on him and becomes angry and aggressive. There is another sudden change of mood when Mick offers Davies the job of caretaker, which Davies accepts. The only snag is that Mick demands references, and Davies says he will get these from Sidcup next day. The scene ends with Davies asking Mick for a pair of shoes to enable him to reach Sidcup.

COMMENTARY:

As with so much in *The Caretaker*, the chasing of Davies by a vacuum cleaner is both comic and frightening, and continues the association between Mick and violent action. Mick's polite and seemingly reasonable explanations of the incident serve only to make it more unsettling. The sight of Davies cowering against the wall with his knife drawn is not attractive; it puts the reader back in the realm of primitive instinct, and the drawn knife has been compared to the fangs that an animal bares when it is threatened or in danger. It has been suggested that Davies is in part a tragic figure, and whilst he is too mean a personality to be convincingly seen in this light, he does have some features that are normally associated with tragic heroes. In this scene it is the ability to bring about his own destruction. He cannot resist the temptation to play off one brother against the other, and so when Mick appears to confide in him, he falls into the trap and starts to be critical of Aston, thinking that this is what Mick wants to hear, and that by dividing the brothers he can dominate the whole house. He should take warning from Mick's sharp reaction, but is unable to do so for very long. There is tremendous irony in the sequence in which Mick talks about his brother being unable to work. Mick says that Aston is 'work shy', or unwilling to work, and Davies says 'I know that sort.' Indeed he does, for he is exactly this type of person himself, and his condemnation of such characters is in fact a condemnation of himself. Mick's offer of the caretaker's job is surprising, but its essential unreality is marked by the fact that it hinges on Davies being able to get his references from Sidcup. The audience are already aware that Davies will never get to Sidcup.

NOTES AND GLOSSARY:

electrolux: the trade name of a brand of vacuum cleaner. Hoover and Thermos are two other company names which have come to mean in common usage all items of a certain type, rather than just the items manufactured by that company

good going over: a thorough clean

house-proud:	very concerned to keep one's home and surroundings neat, clean, and tidy
a start:	a shock, a surprise
spiky:	awkward, ill-tempered
junk:	rubbish, assorted items
playing me about:	playing tricks on me, annoying me
off on the wrong foot:	made a bad start to our relationship
Ay:	Yes
pull anything:	try any tricks, try to deceive me
salt-cellar:	small salt container for table use
make him out:	understand or get to know him
buckle down to the job:	get down to doing some hard work
services:	the armed forces
deeds:	the documents that prove ownership of a property
references:	testimonials
done:	finished, in a mess
pick me up:	find, purchase

Scene 6, page 52: 'Lights up. Morning.'

Aston wakes Davies up, as requested, but on hearing that the weather does not look very promising, Davies immediately gives up his idea of going to Sidcup. Davies stops Aston's complaints about not being able to sleep because of the noise Davies makes at night by complaining himself about the draught from the window on to his bed. Aston says he is going out, but before he does so he starts to speak about a café he used to visit years ago. He used to talk in the café, and at his work in a factory, and have hallucinations. People started to talk about him, and one day he was taken away to a hospital out of London. Against his wishes, Aston's mother signed a form allowing the hospital to operate on Aston's brain; they told him he had a complaint that could only be cured by an operation. Aston tried to escape, but failed. He saw other men being operated on—the doctors put pincers connected to a small machine round the patient's head—and when they came for him he tried to resist. This meant that he was operated on whilst standing up, something which can damage the spine of the patient. Aston's spine is not damaged, but his brain is not the same: he can no longer think clearly, or talk to people as he used to.

COMMENTARY:

Aston's speech is one of the most significant and gripping items in the whole play, and it operates on a number of different levels. On one level, it capitalises on the instinctive fear that normal people have of the mentally ill, using it to disturb and unsettle the audience. However, it is not simply a shock technique, something designed to stimulate an audience and no more. Aston says that he talked too much, and it is possible to see him as a nonconformist, someone who was different from the rest of society, who had to be made to conform, if needs be by means of a brain operation. Stanley, in *The Birthday Party*, is another such figure, someone whose only crime is to be different from other people. The punishment for him, and for Aston, is to have their personality clipped and curtailed, so that they are no longer a threat. The cost of this is that they cease to question, and cease to think.

Perhaps Aston's story is also a criticism of a society that gives everything to the successful, and values material things over everything else, but which discards its casualties with cruel thoughtlessness. Aston is just such a casualty, a man who did not fit into what society saw as being right; and so is Davies. In their different ways, they have been cast off, isolated, and ignored. Yet Aston is the least troubled of the three characters in the play; he has none of Mick's violence, or Davies's bitterness and fear, and in his own way he seems quite content, with only a vague longing in him for what he was, and what he had, before the operation. This is heavily ironical; it is as if Pinter is saying that to be happy and content in society a person has to lose half his mind.

A theme of betrayal is also present in Aston's speech: he has been betrayed by his mother (and possibly Mick too, although his role in the operation is never made clear), when a person's family are the very people in whom he should be able to place absolute trust. However, Pinter has warned his audiences that 'the one thing that people have missed is that it isn't necessary to conclude that everything Aston says about his experiences in the mental hospital is true.' This would seem to suggest that no deep meaning should be read into Aston's speech, and that indeed it may all be a lie. A note of caution, however, needs to be sounded here. Authors who are questioned about their work frequently answer in terms of how they would like their work to be seen, not how it will actually be seen by an audience. If one thing emerges from all Pinter's interviews it is that he has an acute dislike of being pinned down to any one meaning in his work; but this does not mean that the meanings do not exist. It is true to say that no one interpretation to the exclusion of all others can be played on Aston's speech, but that it is a richly evocative and multi-layered dramatic experience, which can be seen in any one of a number of lights.

This leads on to another concern of Pinter's, common to nearly all his plays, that of the nature of truth. The audience are simply not given enough information to enable them to decide if Aston is telling the complete truth, a biased version of a real incident, or a total lie. So in real life people have to rely on words and memory to find out the truth about any situation, and both are subject to alteration by the passing of time, and the urge to see in a situation what the teller wants to see, as distinct from what actually happened. It is not a weakness in *The Caretaker* that the audience may not know how to respond to Aston's speech, but a strength, and a sign of the reality of Pinter's language.

NOTES AND GLOSSARY:

that's shot it:	that has ruined or spoilt my plans
my death of cold:	a severe cold
saw bench:	a metal or wooden bench designed to hold a saw firmly
a minor:	a child. In English law a child cannot be operated on without the written consent of his parents or guardian
put up a fight:	struggle, resist

Act 3, Scene 7, page 58: 'Two weeks later.'

It is two weeks later, and Davies is sitting in a chair with his smoking jacket on, talking to Mick, who is lying on the floor. Davies thinks Aston has mended the leak, but he complains to Mick that Aston will not give him a knife to cut bread with, that he will do nothing about the gas stove, and that he ignores the dirt in the house. Mick does not answer directly, but talks of his dream for the house. He wishes to turn it into a modern, well-decorated 'palace'. Mick asks Davies to explain this to Aston, but Davies declines, saying that he cannot understand Aston, or talk to him effectively. He then complains that he has no clock or way of telling the time. Davies's complaints about Aston become more biting and sharp, and it appears that he is trying to persuade Mick to get rid of Aston, and take Davies on as a partner. Davies asks Mick where he lives, and Mick says he must come to the place for a drink and to listen to some music.

COMMENTARY:

The act opens with Davies and Mick talking in an apparently relaxed and friendly manner, suggesting that Davies is attempting to win over Mick and join in an alliance with him against Aston. Davies's complaints lack substance, and are ridiculous, especially his worries about a gas cooker that is not even connected to the mains; but he cannot resist trying to drive a wedge between the two brothers. In this he is aided by Mick's apparent sympathy, not realising that Mick may well be leading him on into damning himself.

One element emphasised in this scene is the lack of communication between the characters. Davies says of Aston 'He was talking to himself!', and Mick says he cannot communicate adequately with him.

Equally, Mick's euphoric description of a palatial flat is lost on Davies, and Davies does not realise that what he is saying to Mick will eventually result in his being removed from the house. Davies and Mick appear to be talking to each other, whilst in fact they are both talking to themselves, as Aston was when he revealed his experiences in the mental hospital. Davies talks about his sense of grievance, Mick about his dream of a luxury flat, but neither character is able to persuade the other that his personal concern is of any great interest. Mick's description of the flat as it might appear in the future is the direct equivalent of Aston's shed and Davies's papers in Sidcup—a dream that he needs in order to survive in a harsh world, but one which is destined never to be realised. It has been said that this speech is a device to get Davies relaxed, and hence to reveal his true nature to Mick; and also that it is a satire on the jargon of modern, plastic, and synthetic ideas of interior decoration. Davies's desire for a clock emphasises the rootless nature of his existence. He does not need a clock, as he proves when he admits that all it would be useful for is to tell him when his next cup of tea was due; but it expresses his desire to fix himself in time and space, to regulate his life and feel that its progress can be marked in some tangible way. His worry over Aston's smiling at him when he is asleep is pathetic. Davies cannot see that this is a reflection of Aston's need for friendship, not a subtle threat.

NOTES AND GLOSSARY:

chat:	talk
get the hang of him:	understand him
penthouse:	the topmost flat or apartment in a high building, the one directly under the roof
Venetian blinds:	a blind made of thin slats of braid or webbing which can be turned so as to admit or exclude light; they can also be pulled up completely, leaving the window clear
raffia:	thin strips of cured vegetable fibre used to make lamp shades and ornamental items
Clobber:	rubbish, useless material, junk
tuppence:	two pence
foggiest:	faintest
give him a mouthful:	tell him my mind, speak to him firmly
Tchaikovsky:	(1840–93) a famous Russian composer

Scene 8, page 64: 'Davies stands, then goes . . .'

Mick leaves the room before Aston enters, bringing with him a pair of shoes for Davies. Davies complains that they do not fit, and that they

have no laces, but grudgingly accepts the shoes when Aston finds
brown laces for them (the shoes are black). He talks about the job he
has been offered, without mentioning Mick or the house, and about
going down to Sidcup to get his references; but Aston leaves quietly
half-way through the speech, a fact which an angry Davies only realises
some time later.

COMMENTARY:
Davies has been more than willing to take advantage of Aston's kindness and hospitality, but treats the offer of a pair of shoes as if he were
doing Aston a favour by accepting them, and not the other way round.
In effect Davies throws Aston's kindness back in his face, and the
audience are shown the unattractive side of his character. At the end of
the scene, the theme of the preceding scene is re-emphasised. Davies
exclaims 'Christ! That bastard, he ain't even listening to me!' In *The
Caretaker*, people never really listen to one another, only to themselves.
Aston's presence would have made no difference to what Davies said:
what he says is of importance to the speaker, and no one else. Davies
says:

> Maybe they'll get me down to Sidcup tomorrow. If I get down there
> I'll be able to sort myself out.

If he never actually goes to Sidcup, Davies can still persuade himself
that by going there he might be able to 'sort himself out'. If he does go,
it is likely that he will fail to do this, and so his only hope, his illusion,
will be shattered. It is not that Davies does not want to go to Sidcup as
much as the fact that he dare not go; if he goes, it will reveal the hopelessness of his situation. This is clearly seen in the film version of *The
Caretaker*, when at the end of the play Mick offers to drive Davies to
Sidcup in his van, but in the event drops him off after a trip round a
nearby roundabout. Davies is in a state of almost total panic when the
lift to Sidcup is offered. The prospect of facing the truths about himself
that he might find there is too much for him to bear.

NOTES AND GLOSSARY:
do you: fit you
puts the lid on it: stops it from happening
proper: properly
getting on a while back: quite a long time ago

Scene 9, page 66: 'Dim light through the window.'

It is night. Aston wakes Davies up because the noise Davies is making
is stopping Aston from going to sleep. Davies reacts angrily, and abuses

Aston, calling him a mad person and making references to the story Aston told him about the mental hospital and the operation. Davies draws his knife, and Aston says that it is time Davies found somewhere else to live. Davies announces that he has been promised the job of caretaker by Mick, implying that it is Aston who will have to leave the house, not himself. Davies then scorns Aston's dream of building a shed, and Aston tells Davies that he smells. Aston packs Davies's bag for him, and eventually Davies leaves, grumbling, threatening, and complaining.

COMMENTARY:

This scene marks the final break between Aston and Davies, and it is Davies's violent and unpleasant reaction to a justified complaint from Aston that is the most significant element in the scene. Davies is criticised for making a noise in his sleep, and for an unpleasant body odour. The audience know that the former accusation is true, as this scene opens with the stage direction 'DAVIES *groaning*'; and the latter seems credible too. Davies's reaction is to ignore the accusations entirely, and to launch into a heartless and cruel attack on Aston as a person, hitting at his two weak spots: his time in a mental hospital and his cherished dream of a shed. Davies taunts Aston, and insists that he is superior to him, clutching at anything to prove this point. Davies is obeying the law of the jungle, seeking to destroy and humble his opponent without any recourse to reason, logic, or common human decency.

This scene reveals the violence that has been lurking under the surface for much of the duration of *The Caretaker*, and when it does appear, it is both physical and verbal violence. Aston's response to Davies's torrent of abuse is at first surprisingly mild, revealing the hesitant gentleness that is a marked feature of his personality. He says 'I don't think we're hitting it off', a very mild summary of the situation, coming as it does after a knife has been drawn, and vicious assaults have been made on Aston's character. This changes when Davies is rude about Aston's shed. Aston's speech becomes clipped and more threatening, and he says to Davies 'You stink', beginning to exchange insults instead of merely receiving those thrown at him by Davies. He stands firm in the face of Davies's knife, and drives him out of the house despite all his bluster and threats. In order to stay in the house, Davies has revealed the relationship he has with Mick, in the hope that this will suggest he is in a more powerful position than Aston. However, the threat of Mick does not deter Aston, and this foreshadows the end of the play, when the two brothers will unite to reject Davies.

NOTES AND GLOSSARY:

a bit of air: some fresh air

took you in:	committed you to a mental hospital
mucking me about:	inconveniencing me, making a nuisance of yourself
pal:	friend
a creamer:	a mad person, a lunatic
up the creek ... half off!:	mad, insane, mentally unbalanced
nuthouse:	asylum or hospital for the mentally ill
hitting it off:	getting on well with each other, becoming friends

---

Scene 10, page 70: 'Lights up. Early evening.'

Davies and Mick enter the room, talking. Mick appears to sympathise with Davies's complaints about Aston, although he reacts strangely when Davies makes references to his brother's mental illness. Mick becomes angry when Davies says that he is not an experienced interior decorator. Mick insists that he said he was, and says he will not offer him a job or a home. Davies says that Aston is mad, and Mick turns on him, describes him as a 'wild animal', and gives him some money to go away. In a rage, Mick hurls Aston's Buddha against the gas cooker, smashing it in pieces. He says Aston can have the house and do what he likes with it. There is silence.

COMMENTARY:
The arrival of Mick and Davies, apparently on friendly terms with each other, gives a false impression to the audience that Davies might succeed in replacing Aston in the house. Such false impressions, and sudden reversals, are a favourite technique of Pinter's. Mick's assertion that Davies is a qualified interior decorator comes as a complete surprise, both to Davies and the audience, and it shocks Davies into complaining that Aston is 'nutty', or mentally unbalanced. This provokes Mick into making a verbal assault on Davies:

> Every word you speak is open to any number of different interpretations. Most of what you say is lies. You're violent, you're erratic, you're just completely unpredictable. You're nothing else but a wild animal, when you come down to it.

Much of this is true, and Mick's reference to a wild animal repeats a description of himself that Davies has used earlier. There is also irony in this speech; many of the features that Mick isolates could equally well apply to him, as he too is violent, erratic, and unpredictable. His sharp response to the suggestion that his brother is mentally ill raises the question of the role he played in his brother's operation. His sensitivity could be seen as the result of a guilty conscience; equally, it could spring from a mutual desire to defend and protect his brother, or from shame at having a relation with mental illness. Davies's anguished plea

'Won't you listen to what I'm saying?' repeats earlier lines that show characters desperate to communicate, but apparently talking only to themselves. The theme of the family cannot be ignored in this scene. The line that finally seals Davies's fate comes when Mick says 'What did you call my brother?' The emphasis here comes on the words 'my brother', and it has been suggested that this is a 'primal cry', the surfacing of a basic family relationship that is instinctive and unbreakable by any outsider such as Davies. It is also possible to see Davies as a representative of primitive man, attempting to break into the tribal group formed by Aston and Mick, and dominate it.

Many critics have commented on the significance of the smashing of the Buddha statue. It is perplexing: the audience know that the statue is valued by Aston, and Mick has just been defending him. It seems illogical for him at this moment to break something that is held in esteem by his brother. However, immediately after he hurls it against the gas cooker, Mick seems to be denying responsibility for Aston, and any interest in him. He says:

> He can do it up, he can decorate it, he can do what he likes with it. I'm not bothered. I thought I was doing him a favour, letting him live here. He's got his own ideas. Let him have them. I'm going to chuck it in.

Mick says 'I've got to think about the future', and the audience might feel that he is doing this in order to stop thinking about the present, something which all the characters do in *The Caretaker*. The smashing of the Buddha need not be seen as a major symbol, but simply as an expression of an inner fury in Mick, a tension and violence in his nature that has been hinted at throughout the play.

NOTES AND GLOSSARY:

sort him out: put him on the right track, make him do the right thing

sense: intelligence, ability

en he?: hasn't he?

sitting tenant: British law gives a sitting tenant (someone who is living in rented accommodation) certain rights of tenure

notice: advance warning of eviction from rented accommodation

furnished . . . unfurnished: the law as it applies to tenanted accommodation is different when the house or room is provided with furniture from what it is when let unfurnished

turn my hand: apply myself, manage to do

pick it up: learn it

nutty:	insane, mentally unbalanced
half a dollar:	two shillings and sixpence, or twelve and a half new pence
chuck it in:	give it up

Scene 11, page 75: 'Aston comes in.'

Aston enters, and he and Mick smile at each other. After a few incoherent words, Mick leaves. Davies explains that he came back for his pipe, and Aston goes to the plug he has been mending for most of the play, and starts to work on it with a screwdriver. Davies tries to make Aston take him in again, suggesting that they change beds, but Aston refuses. Davies tries again, this time offering to help with the shed that Aston plans to build, but again is refused. Davies pleads with him incoherently to be allowed to stay, but Aston remains silent.

COMMENTARY:
There is something strangely sinister in the smile that Aston and Mick exchange at the start of this scene, although its meaning, if any, is never made clear. Perhaps it is best seen as a sign of the understanding that they have, which dooms Davies to being an outsider in their relationship. Davies's pleading with Aston is pathetic, and some critics have seen his expulsion from the house as being a representation of mankind's banishment from Paradise. This is an attractive idea, but cannot be taken too far, if for no other reason than that no one was left in Paradise after the expulsion of Adam and Eve in the Old Testament story, whereas Aston, and to a certain extent Mick, remain the inhabitants of the house in *The Caretaker*. The height of pathos is achieved when Davies asks plaintively 'What shall I do . . . Where am I going to go?' His clumsy attempts to play one brother off against the other have resulted in him losing everything, and the chance is gone forever. Pinter originally considered having Davies killed at the end of the play, but realised that this was not necessary; the effect is complete without this further violence, and much of the pathos of the ending comes about as a result of the helplessness of Davies, the fact that he is left to survive in a world on his own, away from the relative comfort and security he has found with Aston. He cries 'But you don't understand my meaning' to Aston, emphasising again the theme of lack of communication and understanding between people in the play.

NOTES AND GLOSSARY:
yourn:	yours
get up:	erect, build
I'll give you a hand:	I'll help you

Part 3

Commentary

NEARLY AS MANY words have been written on the works of Harold Pinter as have been written by Pinter himself. This booming critical industry based on the author can present a problem for the student, who could very easily find himself faced with at least ten different critical interpretations of *The Caretaker*. Furthermore, even the most charitable reader will find that some of the things written about Pinter are more difficult and obscure than the original works they are meant to clarify. A further problem is that Pinter has been widely interviewed, and some of his own remarks on his works are readily available to the student. This should, of course, be a help rather than a hindrance, but Pinter's remarks are sometimes contradictory, and often intentionally non-committal. At the best of times, what an author says about his work needs to be treated with a mixture of respect and caution, because an author will often tell an interviewer what he intended his work to achieve, rather than being able to comment on what it actually has achieved. The final problem is that *The Caretaker* does not fit into any neat category, as is the case with some older works of literature. It is neither comedy nor tragedy, but a mixture of these and many other elements which combine into what is essentially a new form of drama, albeit one with many links to past plays and authors. There are two tendencies which should be firmly resisted by the student: the first is to believe that Pinter never made mistakes in his plays, and the second is to treat Pinter as a philosopher, instead of a dramatist very concerned with the mechanics of live theatre.

Themes

The theme of a work of literature is the idea or ideas that an author chooses to examine in his work. There are any number of themes in *The Caretaker*, with critics seeming to find new ones almost every year. This is partly a result of Pinter's style and approach. He does not preach, lecture, or make categorical statements, but instead presents his audiences with incidents, characters, and language that suggest something of great significance is taking place, without always being specific about what it is. This unwillingness to be pinned down to a definitive statement, or to tell his audiences clearly what his plays are about, has led to Pinter being criticised for obscurity, and even to him being called a theatrical fraud. It has been said that his plays are hollow shells: works which appear on the surface to have meaning, but on close examination prove to be empty and meaningless. Pinter has been accused of deliberately mystifying events in his plays, in order to gain a rather cheap theatrical suspense.

Much of this criticism is unfair. Whilst Pinter's plays neither have a definite moral, nor state explicitly the conclusions an audience should draw from them, there is no law which states that a work of literature must do these things. Pinter's plays are exploratory; they stimulate their audience into thought on a wide range of topics, and on a number of different levels, but leave the audience to draw their own conclusions from this experience. *The Caretaker* can be linked to a wide range of ideas and suggestions, and this is a measure of its skill in evoking a wide-ranging response. Interpretations of it are parallel: it is at one and the same time a play about loneliness and isolation, about personal identity, about communication between people, and about human nature. It can comment on all these things, and many more, at the same time, and it is wrong to seek for a single meaning. Its greatest attributes are its richness and diversity. Thus the themes listed below are not a complete list of possible interpretations of *The Caretaker*, and the sensitive student will be able to provide a number of additional interpretations of his own. Nor are these themes mutually exclusive; belief in one does not mean rejection of another.

Loneliness, isolation, and the outcast

Characters in Pinter's plays are very often lonely, either by choice or because their personality does not allow them to form satisfactory relationships. Loneliness is one of the themes of *The Caretaker*, and it is a theme that is expressed largely through the characters of Davies and Aston.

Davies is alone when Aston rescues him from the brawl at the café, and after a brief interlude he is left alone again at the end of the play. One of the sad ironies of the play is that he realises his isolation and how much the companionship of the house has meant to him only when it is too late, and he has destroyed the chance of ending that isolation. He says to Aston:

> You been a good friend to me. You took me in. You took me in, you didn't ask me no questions, you give me a bed, you been a mate to me.

Davies is an outcast, a vagrant, someone cut off from society, and Pinter leaves his audience in no doubt that his isolation is a terrible thing. Yet Pinter's double-edged vision means that the audience are not presented simply with a character deserving their sympathy. They are shown just as clearly that at least some of this isolation is self-imposed. Davies is aggressive, truculent, and unstable. He is embittered, full of racial prejudice, almost completely selfish, and lacking any sense of loyalty and gratitude. On a more practical level, he does 'stink', and he keeps Aston awake with his groaning and noise at night. In short, he is a thoroughly unpleasant person, and the audience are stopped short in their rush of sympathy for Davies by these facts. The result is a complex reaction whereby pity is mingled with an awareness that Davies's isolation is inevitable, given who and what he is.

Aston is a different case. He too is lonely:

> But I don't talk to people now. I steer clear of places like that café. I never go into them now. I don't talk to anyone . . . like that.

His offer to Davies of a room and a job, and his kindness towards him, suggest a man desperate for human companionship, as isolated and lonely in his way as Davies is in his. Yet Aston's isolation is not as simple as that of Davies, and springs from a different cause. Davies trusts no one, and turns on those who try to help him, as when he tries to join Mick in an alliance against Aston. In rejecting him society is doing no more than paying him back in his own coin. But Aston's fault seems to have been exactly the opposite; he seems to have trusted people too much:

> But they always used to listen. I thought . . . they understood what I said. I mean I used to talk to them. I talked too much. That was my mistake. The same in the factory.

His reward for this trust was to be betrayed by his mother, and be forced to undergo a loathsome operation on his brain. He trusted too much, Davies not at all, but the result is the same for both—isolation and loneliness.

The saddest irony of all is that although both characters need the companionship that is at least present in potential in their relationship, they are unable to realise it. It is almost as if Pinter is saying that humans are destined to be lonely, and the more they cry out for an end to this, the more its certainty is assured. There is, of course, one major difference between the two characters: Davies is completely alone, but Aston has his brother, a relationship that seems indissoluble, and resists Davies's assaults on it with comparative ease. Yet doubts are thrown even on this type of relationship, the one based on family, by the 'treachery' of Aston's mother, the hints that Mick might also have betrayed Aston in allowing the operation to proceed, and his apparent willingness in Act 3 to leave Aston to his own devices:

He can do it up, he can decorate it, he can do what he likes with it. I'm
not bothered. I thought I was doing him a favour, letting him live
here. He's got his own ideas. Let him have them. I'm going to chuck
it in.

It is possible to read a variety of meanings into the presentation of
loneliness in the play, but simple answers should be treated with
caution. It can be suggested that *The Caretaker* is a simple moral tale,
showing how loneliness is an inevitable companion of selfishness, and
how the generosity that Davies lacks is the only sure way to gain friend-
ships and for humans to live together in society; but straightforward
interpretations such as this crumble on closer examination. Davies is
selfish and lacks generosity, but it is not possible to say from this that
his isolation is his own fault. His selfishness and lack of generosity
could be the result of his not being shown any himself by other people,
so that he has been unable to learn how to exercise these virtues. He is a
relatively old man when he meets Aston, perhaps too old to start this
learning process. If his faults are an inevitable result of his own bad
treatment by other people, then the isolation that results is the fault of
the other people, not his own.

Aston is equally lonely and isolated, but he is generous and unselfish;
so for him the argument does not work. Perhaps the only clear thing
that can be seen in the play is a statement that people need friendship
and fear isolation; only very great fear and need could produce such
pathetic pleading for a place in the house as that uttered by Davies at the
end of the play. *The Caretaker* presents loneliness as one of the horrors
of modern life.

Communication

Loneliness and communication, or the lack of it, are closely linked. The
characters in *The Caretaker*, and most other plays by Pinter, have a
desperate yearning to communicate with their fellows, but time and
time again are thwarted in this desire. The words go out from the mouth
of the speaker, but either fail to arrive, or fail to say what is meant. Thus
one of the major themes in *The Caretaker* is the inadequacy of communication between people. Pinter himself pointed to one aspect of this
theme in a lecture entitled 'Writing for the Theatre' which he delivered
at Bristol in 1962:

> I think we communicate only too well, in our silence, in what is unsaid,
> and that what takes place is continual evasion, desperate rearguard
> attempts to keep ourselves to ourselves. Communication is too
> alarming. To enter into someone else's life is too frightening. To dis-
> close to others the poverty within us is too fearsome a possibility.

Pinter is saying here that more can be learnt from what is not said than from what is. Conversation and words are a barrier, a defence erected to stop others perceiving a person's real nature, because often that nature is weak and deficient, and the owner frightened to reveal it. A person does not state what he is when he talks, but what he would like others to think he is. Certainly in *The Caretaker* silence can communicate just as effectively as words. The play ends with Davies's words becoming fewer and fewer, and the silences longer, until the final silence that closes the play,

> Listen . . . if I . . . got down . . . if I was to . . . get my papers . . . would you . . . would you let . . . would you . . . if I got down . . . and got my . . .
> *Long silence*
> *Curtain*

It is the silence, not the words, that reveals the final breakdown of communication between Aston and Davies, the hopelessness of Davies's position, and the limbo into which he will soon be thrust.

The audience can also hear numerous examples of Davies using language to hide what he really is, to present a false picture of his character in the manner suggested by Pinter in his lecture. His repeated references to his papers down in Sidcup suggest that he is a person with a purpose in life, not the rootless vagabond that he really is. His pleading for a clock is meant to hide the fact that he is really a man without purpose, and that time is irrelevant to him. His comments on the dirtiness of coloured people are an attempt to divert attention away from his own filth and smell, and when he says that he has 'had dinner with the best' he is attempting to claim a familiarity with high society that he clearly lacks. Much of Davies's language is therefore 'continual evasion', an attempt to hide the 'poverty' within him. It fails because the audience can weigh what is said against what they see, and quickly realise that what Davies says often means exactly the opposite of what is the truth.

Mick uses language not to communicate with people, but to confuse and mislead them. His lists of people of whom Davies reminds him and London streets, his torrent of decorating terms and legal jargon, all act as an effective barrier to his true meaning, and the real nature of his personality. It is a much more sophisticated barrier than that of Davies, and far harder to penetrate. Both characters say a lot in the play, but the audience feel they know much more by the end of the play about Davies than they do about Mick. Yet even in Mick's speeches a clear feeling of hostility towards Davies emerges, a feeling that on the surface at least bears little relationship to what he actually says.

Mick says to Davies 'Every word you speak is open to any number of interpretations', and this is certainly a theme of the play. Words can mean nothing, or be subject to a number of wildly different interpretations. When Mick says of his brother 'No, he just doesn't like work, that's his trouble', he could be making a genuine criticism of Aston, but equally he could be luring Davies into a trap, commenting on Davies, or expressing his own guilt about what was done to Aston. It may be that he is doing all these things, a pointer to the complexity of response that even the simplest phrases in *The Caretaker* sometimes demand of the reader.

Yet despite the fact that language is used by the characters in *The Caretaker* to confuse more than to communicate, Pinter allows each of his characters at least one speech in which they reveal a part of their true selves, where something central and vital to their character and sense of identity is said. Aston's monologue about the hospital and his operation, Davies's speech where he states 'you been a good friend to me', and to a certain extent Mick's dream of a decorated flat are some of the most striking examples. In these speeches something of vital importance to the individual characters is being expressed, and nowhere can this be seen more clearly than in this speech by Davies:

> Don't know as these shoes'll be much good. It's a hard road, I been down there before. Coming the other way, like. Last time I left there, it was . . . last time . . . getting on a while back . . . the road was bad, the rain was coming down, lucky I didn't die there on the road, but I got here, I kept going, all along . . . yes . . . I kept going all along. But all the same, I can't go on like this, what I got to do, I got to get back there, find this man—
> *He turns and looks about the room.*
> Christ! That bastard, he ain't even listening to me!

In this speech Davies comes face to face with the misery and struggle of his existence, and makes the ultimate admission that 'I can't go on like this'. It is a moment of intense truth and self-recognition, and there is only one other time in the play when the audience see straight into his soul in this manner, and where Davies speaks stripped of all pretence and deception. This is in the final scene, where he pleads to be allowed to stay in the house. Pinter has written about moments like these:

> I am not suggesting that no character in a play can ever say what he in fact means. Not at all. I have found that there invariably does come a moment when this happens, when he says something, perhaps, which he has never said before. And where this happens, what he says is irrevocable, and can never be taken back.

Yet the final line of Davies's speech ('he ain't even listening to me!') points to another truth about these moments of intensity: no one listens.

Aston leaves the room half-way through what Davies is saying; and when Aston speaks about his experiences, Davies is in shadow, and Aston appears almost to be speaking to himself. All Davies can remember of this speech is the fact of Aston's stay in a mental hospital and the pincers, and it is as if he has not heard the rest of it. Mick's description of the house as it might be is lost on Davies, who can understand neither the technical terms nor Mick's enthusiasm. Thus the final irony is that when characters do say something revealing and worthy of communication, it is as if they are speaking to themselves. No one listens, but everybody talks a great deal; and perhaps this is the most significant statement made in *The Caretaker*.

Primitive instincts and survival

Pinter's plays often show fairly normal people conversing, meeting, and going about their business with every outward sign of normality, but the audience are made aware that beneath the surface of these exchanges a basic battle of dominance is taking place. Nowhere is this more clearly seen than in the figure of Davies. Aston and the room offer him the security and base that he so desperately needs, but it is as if there is a basic instinct at work in him that will not allow the situation to be left as it stands. He must try to play Mick off against Aston, and achieve the position of dominance in the house. Equally, Mick seems determined not to let an intruder into the house, and views his house as an animal would view its territory, as something not to be impinged on by an outsider. For Davies, the result is rejection, and further misery, and what makes the episode even sadder is that he lacks the self-knowledge to realise how this has come about, and so avoid its occurrence in the future.

The picture of human nature that Pinter presents is not a pleasant one. He seems to be suggesting that beneath the civilised exterior of people there lurks a basic savagery, a primitive instinct for domination and control over territory, that makes a mockery of so-called civilised man. Thus Davies twice draws his knife, like an animal baring its fangs, and is referred to as a 'wild animal' by Mick. However, Mick's behaviour is hardly more laudable. He takes a delight in terrifying and confusing Davies, and the manner in which he leads Davies on to a revelation of his true nature is like a hunter using his intelligence against an animal in the wild.

Social criticism

There is a theme of social criticism in *The Caretaker*, but like all the play's themes, it is illusive and difficult to pin down. On one level,

Davies is a man rejected by society because he does not have his 'papers'. Without the documentary evidence by which society labels and categorises its members, he is a lost soul; society does not recognise an individual, only a name and number on a piece of paper, and without these papers the individual does not exist. So Davies is condemned to wander rootless and unwanted, terrified by vague fears of persecution. He cannot cope with the technical terms that Mick throws at him, the references to house owning and purchase, insurance, and banking; but a knowledge of such things is the price society demands of its would-be inhabitants. Without papers, Davies is a man without identity, a lost soul destined to be forever denied a sense of belonging.

Davies is one of society's casualties, and the manner in which he is treated by society gives little hope of it being a caring or wise entity. Aston is also a casualty, but in his case it is possible to see a further statement contained in the story of what has happened to him. Pinter never says what he was before his operation; all the audience hear is that he talked to people, and talked too much. He could have been a political revolutionary, an industrial activist, or simply a dissident, someone not prepared to accept immediately and without question what society asked him to believe. His operation can thus be seen as society's retribution, and a symbol of the fear in which it holds the person who is a potential threat to it. Any such threat must be cruelly and immediately destroyed, in this case by taking away Aston's ability to think. The result is a man who will not pose any threat to the established way of things; but a terrible price has been paid, namely the loss of all that made Aston a distinct individual. In Davies, Pinter shows his audience how society treats its rejects; in Aston, he shows them how it creates them.

Racial prejudice also is highlighted in *The Caretaker*, through the medium of Davies, and is revealed as the height of folly. Davies's hatred of coloured people is simply a cover for his own deficiencies, and his fear of them is irrational. He is a total failure, a wreck of a man, but by criticising coloured people he can persuade himself that he is at least superior to someone, and gain solace from this illusion. Equally the 'Blacks' are conveniently there to be blamed for anything that goes wrong; even the noise Davies makes in the night is their fault, not his own. They are the perfect scapegoat, people who can be blamed for anything and so divert attention away from the real object of blame. Racial prejudice allows Davies to blame others for what is actually his own fault.

Perhaps Mick's dream of a 'penthouse' flat is also an implied criticism of society. Mick's greatest aim in life seems to be to bring the house up to the standards that modern society finds desirable. In Act 3 he says:

I'd have teal-blue, copper and parchment linoleum squares. I'd have those colours re-echoed in the walls. I'd offset the kitchen units with charcoal-grey worktops. Plenty of room for cupboards for the crockery. We'd have a small wall-cupboard, a large wall-cupboard, a corner wall-cupboard with revolving shelves. You wouldn't be short of cupboards.

All this decoration will change the appearance of the house, but its basic structure will remain the same, as will the people inside it. What Mick wants is to coat the surface of the house, but go no deeper. Such an aim is made to appear trivial, a false value, in a play that deals with major human problems such as isolation, communication, and prejudice.

The room

In nearly all Pinter's early plays the theme of 'the room' makes an appearance. The audience are shown a person who has retreated into a house or room and there created a haven of peace and security, cut off and isolated from the outside world, and therefore not threatened by it. Inevitably the outside world, or a representative of it, breaks into the room, destroying its isolation and its inhabitant. In *The Caretaker* this position is reversed. The centre of interest is not someone inside the room trying to keep out the world, but an outsider trying to enter.

Despite this difference, the room in *The Caretaker* is similar in many respects to the rooms in other Pinter plays. It stands for security and warmth, somewhere where Aston and Davies can keep the outside world at bay, and indulge in their respective dreams. It helps to show the outside world as a threatening place, and man's need for a safe haven within it.

The room also acts as an emblem for the state of Aston's mind. It is full of 'clobber' and 'junk', a bizarre mixture of valuable and valueless items, unorganised and in disarray. Just as Aston cannot clear and organise the room, so his mind is in disarray, cluttered and confused. However, in one respect the room in *The Caretaker* cannot be compared with the rooms or houses in other plays by Pinter. In a play such as *The Birthday Party* all the threat comes from outside the house in which Stanley lives, in the form of the two gangsters Goldberg and McCann; whereas in *The Caretaker* the threat comes from within the room, in the shape of Mick. Perhaps for this reason Davies could be described as the most desperate of Pinter's characters; the others are at least able to find a temporary peace and security in a room, but for Davies the threat to his security appears in the room almost as soon as he enters it.

Dreams and illusions

All three characters in *The Caretaker* have a dream or hope for the future: something they are going to do which will in some manner make their lives more acceptable and worthwhile. Davies is going to Sidcup, Aston is going to build his shed, and Mick is going to decorate the house. In each case the audience are led to feel that these dreams will never be realised, that they will come to nothing, which leads on to the question of why they are necessary to the characters concerned.

Life is not very attractive for the characters in *The Caretaker*. Davies is a dirty and miserable tramp, rejected and homeless, a person of no consequence to anyone other than himself. Aston has been reduced to a shadow of his former self by an operation; and whilst Mick appears to have energy and drive, he seems unable actually to do any of the things he wants to, and even he is driven to express a desire to 'chuck it all in'. In the face of bleak prospects and a mundane day-to-day existence, each character has found a dream. It does not matter if these dreams are impossible and will never be realised. What does matter is that each character feels that his dream might take place. The dream is an illusion, since it is not based on anything firmer than a desire for it to be true, but to the characters it is more substantial. It gives hope to all of them, hope which otherwise they would be denied, and is therefore an essential part of their adaptation to life. Davies makes his biggest mistake when he refers to Aston's 'stinking shed', and implies that it will never be built. This produces one of the few instances in the play when Aston responds in a violent and incisive manner, defying Davies's knife and effectively driving him out of the room and house. Similarly, in the film version of the play, Davies is reduced to absolute panic when Mick offers to drive him down to Sidcup. The point about these dreams is that they crumble and are destroyed if the cold wind of reality brushes them. To test them in real life is to show up cruelly and remorselessly how unreal they are, and to take away from the character the one thing that makes life bearable.

The whole identity of Davies and Aston has become bound up with and even based on their dreams, and a threat to the dream is a threat to this identity. This can be seen even more clearly in *The Birthday Party* when Goldberg and McCann force Stanley into the real world, not allowing him to hold on to his dream that he is a skilled concert pianist. The result is that Stanley is reduced to an incoherent, empty shell of a human being. With his dream gone, his illusion, there is nothing else. Pinter spares his characters this ultimate destruction in *The Caretaker*. They still have their dreams at the end of the play, battered though they are; but the audience are in no doubt that to remove their cherished illusions would be to destroy the personality. Pinter seems to be saying that to survive, a person must cut himself off from reality, and live in a world of dreams and illusions; real life is too bitter to allow survival.

Other themes

There have been some rather wild critical interpretations of *The Caretaker*. At least two critics have seen it as a semi-religious allegory, with Davies as Everyman and Aston and Mick representing the forces of good and evil. Pinter has resisted such interpretations with some fierceness, reputedly saying 'It's about two brothers and a caretaker.' Such interpretations are far too neat for a Pinter play, and deny the complexity and richness of multiple interpretation which is Pinter's main strength.

Another interpretation suggests that the play is about the conflict between different generations. Davies is a father-figure, and his rejection at the end of the play a symbol of the manner in which the older generation must be made to stand aside for the younger. Up to this point the interpretation has considerable value, but it becomes rather less convincing when extended into suggestions that Davies's unthinking feeling of superiority to Aston is like that of a father to a son, and that Aston in the grip of the psychiatrists is like a child under the tyrannical rule of overbearing parents. However, the two brothers are a family unit, and there are hints in *The Caretaker* of an interest in the way that families react and interact that reaches its greatest fulfilment in Pinter's next major play, *The Homecoming*.

As usual in a Pinter play, women do not emerge with any great credit from *The Caretaker*. All the characters are male, but the women who are mentioned (Aston's mother, the girl who propositions Aston in the café) are hardly praiseworthy.

The theme of menace is ever-present in Pinter's earlier plays, and in *The Caretaker*, though to a lesser degree. It is arguable that this is not a theme so much as just a presence in the play. Davies feels menaced by a host of things which he does not understand, such as National Insurance and a disconnected gas cooker. He is clearly menaced by Mick in a more obvious fashion, whilst Mick himself may be frightened of losing his brother to Davies. Aston cannot forget his experiences in hospital, and his silences can be menacing once the audience know that they emanate from a character whose mind has been affected and whose responses are not as predictable as those of an ordinary person. The story of Aston being taken away to hospital against his wishes and tortured there into conformity suggests a hostile outside world waiting to pounce on those it suspects of dissidence.

The play also shows another Pinter concern, the difficulty of establishing what is truth. The audience do not know whether what Aston

says about his experiences is the truth or a fantasy; they have no way of
knowing if Davies ever did have any papers, or if they were left in Sidcup; they quickly learn not to trust anything Mick says, and his sudden
accusation that Davies said he was an experienced decorator is impossible for Davies to disprove. All he has available is his remembrance of
words that were spoken, and both memory and words are fallible and
unreliable. As Mick says, towards the end of Act 3, 'Every word . . .
is open to any number of interpretations', and when this is the case,
and human beings have only their memory to go by, distinguishing
truth from imagination, fact from fiction, becomes an almost impossible
task.

Characters

Davies

Davies is an old man, probably in his sixties. He wears shabby clothing,
is never seen to wash, is presumably dirty, and is accused of having an
unpleasant smell. He is full of resentment at his lowly position in life,
and at the way people treat him 'like dirt', and he expresses this resentment by an illogical hatred of 'Blacks, Greeks, Poles, the lot of them'.
He is servile when he stands to gain from it, calling Aston 'mister' in
Act 1, but is also insecure about his lowly status, as is seen when he tries
to convince Aston that he has 'had dinner with the best'. Equally, he is
extremely sensitive about who is 'superior' to him, and whilst servile to
those in authority resents bitterly the attempt of the 'Scotch git' who was
'not my boss' to give him orders.

A rootless wanderer of no account to anyone, he is pathetically keen
to establish that he has 'rights', and perhaps one point that Pinter makes
through his portrayal of Davies is that all humans, however lowly their
position, do have the right to a certain decency and humanity of treatment. If this is a theme, it is qualified by an awareness that Davies has a
vicious streak in him. About the Scotsman who attacked him he says,
'One night I'll get him. When I find myself around that direction'; and
this suggestion of viciousness is amplified later in the play when he twice
draws his knife, and when he cruelly taunts Aston about his experiences
in the mental hospital (Aston being the only person to have shown him
any kindness):

> They can put the pincers on your head again, man! They can have
> them on again! Any time. All they got to do is get the word. They'd
> carry you in there, boy. They'd come here and pick you up and carry
> you in! They'd keep you fixed! They'd put them pincers on your
> head, they'd have you fixed!

In this speech the 'mister' has been replaced by the somewhat offensive 'man' and 'boy', and Davies appears to be enjoying what he is saying, rejoicing in his superiority over Aston and gloating over his troubles.

Davies is more than prepared to beg, as is shown by his request to Aston for some shoes, and the story of his visit to the monastery; but when his requests are refused his cringing quickly turns to abuse. He seems disgusted that the monks treated him like an animal, but unaware that this is all he really is. Davies says he has been going around under the assumed name of Bernard Jenkins, but that 'papers' which will prove his real name of Mac Davies are in Sidcup. His journey to Sidcup to pick up his papers is a continual theme of his conversation, and its significance has already been noted. Davies groans in his sleep, but when told of this denies it fiercely, just as he vehemently denies all criticism, blaming the 'Blacks' in the rest of the house. Davies trusts no one, and assumes that others feel the same way about him; he is therefore surprised when Aston is prepared to leave him alone in the room. He has no knowledge of civilised living, as is shown by his belief that a disconnected gas cooker could poison him. Later in the play he is reduced to terror by Mick's list of legal, technical, and insurance terms, revealing himself as someone totally unable to cope with the paraphernalia of modern living. Mick describes him as 'choosy', which he certainly is. He will not take the shoes that Aston offers him, and refuses two shirts for illogical reasons. Yet at the same time he accepts a smoking jacket, which will be of much less use to him than the shirts. This behaviour is illogical; but it is true to human nature. It has been shown that families on low incomes in the 1930s in Great Britain could obtain medically satisfactory diets, but refused the opportunity to do so, and purchased jam and luxury foods instead. The reason for this was that the luxury items, though not essential in a strictly practical sense, did give a hint of a different style of life, and enlivened the boredom of a strictly functional diet. So although the smoking jacket is not a necessity for Davies, its very luxury makes it attractive to him; to have something non-essential lets Davies think that he has clothes to spare—an illusion, but a pleasant one. Mick calls him an 'old rogue' and an 'old scoundrel', both accurate descriptions. Davies has a fear of the outside world and 'them', the people who will come to check up on his papers, if there is a bell and a door marked 'Caretaker' downstairs. He is easily terrified by a vacuum cleaner in the dark, having no knowledge of machines like this, and reveals his animal savagery in his reaction to this incident, where he draws a knife on Mick. When established in the house, Davies starts to complain, about not having a knife, a clock, or a draught-free bed, and about Aston. On Aston's story of his experiences in the mental hospital he says:

> He went on talking there . . . I don't know what he was . . . he wasn't
> looking at me, he wasn't talking to me, he don't care about me. He
> was talking to himself!

This, of course, is all characters ever do in *The Caretaker*, but a realisation of this fact is beyond Davies. He is himself anguished when later
Aston does not listen to him, crying out when he realises 'Christ! That
bastard, he ain't even listening to me!'

Davies is no judge of character. He believes that Mick is 'straightforward', and is terrified of Aston smiling at him; whereas in fact it is
Aston whom he should trust, and Mick who poses the greatest threat.
As Mick says, 'You get a bit out of your depth sometimes, don't you?',
and nowhere is this more so than in his dealings with Aston and Mick.
Davies's desire to dominate, and his lack of generosity and flexibility,
are what cause him to be banished from the house. In addition his lack
of awareness of other people allows him to say things to Mick and
Aston that they cannot forgive: he describes Aston's shed as 'stinking',
and tells Mick that his brother is a 'nutter'. He is reduced to pathetic
pleading at the end of the play, but it is to no avail.

Davies is an expert at self-deception. He is incapable of seeing himself
as he really is, perhaps because if he did the vision would be so hopeless
and depressing that he would give up. Thus his self-deception and lack
of self-knowledge are not simply wilful ignorance, but something vital
to his survival, and a means of hiding from the truth that might otherwise kill him. Pinter raises an interesting point: whether or not it is fair
to ask for self-knowledge from someone when it is tantamount to self-
destruction. Davies is also extremely selfish, and the combination of
selfishness and lack of self-knowledge stops him from seeing what other
people are like, as well as rendering him incapable of generosity.

The reader must decide for himself whether or not he retains any
sympathy for Davies. On the one hand, he is shown as a repulsive and
loathsome member of humanity who gets what he deserves; on the
other hand, it is impossible not to feel at least the stirrings of pity for him
(especially at the end of the play) and that his treatment at the hands of
others may be responsible for the way that he himself treats other people.
He is lazy, ill-tempered, quarrelsome, bitter, violent, and selfish; and
these features have led to him being seen as an attack on the British
working man, and on racially prejudiced people. His urge to dominate
the room has been seen as an allegory of original sin, a sign that man is
inherently evil and sinful; and also as part of a portrayal of primitive
man, suggesting that our primitive natures lie just under the surface of
our civilised behaviour. Whatever the symbolic meaning, you should
notice one other feature of his portrayal—its realism. One critic has
hailed him as 'the first truly realistic bum in the history of English

literature' ('bum' being in this instance an American slang term denoting a tramp, vagabond, beggar, or ne'er do well). Whatever else he might or might not be, Davies has the taste of reality about him, in itself no small triumph on Pinter's part.

Aston

Aston is in his late twenties or early thirties, and wears a shabby pinstriped suit that was given to him at the hospital. This form of clothing is often associated with conformity and respectability, and has led to suggestions that Aston is a representative of the artist in society (someone who 'talks too much'), and that because society cannot tolerate the artistic personality it reduced him to conformity, and the outward symbol of this is the suit. This is certainly a possible interpretation, but it owes a great deal to the fact that Stanley in *The Birthday Party*, a character much more readily identifiable as an artist persecuted by society, is also given a suit as a symbol of his enforced conformity and respectability. Certainly Aston describes his problem as being too sensitive; he cherishes a statue of Buddha; and he says that he talked too much. All these might suggest an artistic personality, but could equally well suggest over-sensitivity without artistic ability, a search for a religion or meaning in life, and a political or industrial activist. Perhaps the safest way to interpret Aston before his operation is to see him simply as a nonconformist and dissident personality, without being any more specific than this.

Aston is generous. He rescues Davies from the café, places a chair for him, offers him a room and a bed, goes back for his bag, and finds him another when the original one is unobtainable. He gives Davies a cigarette, a pair of shoes, money, and the bag. He speaks most often in monosyllables, and in this sense his long speech about his hospital experience is out of character. However, this is a strength in his portrayal, rather than a weakness, for the length of his speech suggests how important the experience has been for him, if it can draw out of him so many words; though there are other times when Aston says more than just a sentence or a few words:

> I went into a pub the other day. Ordered a Guinness. They gave it to me in a thick mug. I sat down but I couldn't drink it. I can't drink Guinness from a thick mug. I only like it out of a thin glass. I had a few sips but I couldn't finish it.

This speech has been interpreted as a sign of Aston's sensitivity, but this view is of doubtful validity. It may show him to be sensitive, but this is not its main impact. The most noticeable feature is its inconsequentiality and strangeness. It bears no relation to what Davies has just been saying, and is not followed up by either character. What it does is unnerve the audience. It is irrational and illogical, creating interest and tension simply through its unexpectedness. It suggests a mind following its own course, regardless of what is taking place around it. It may also be a superhuman effort on Aston's part to make polite conversation. It comes after a pause, when the conversation seems to have come to a halt. Perhaps Aston is frightened of the silence, or perhaps he feels that good manners demand more of a contribution from him than he has been providing up to this point. Both interpretations are possible.

Aston says he is good with his hands, and likes to work with them, but he is still meddling with the same plug at the end of the play as he was at the start, without appearing to have come any nearer to correcting its fault. Similarly, the shed is talked about, but no move is made towards its completion. It has been suggested that Aston becomes more confident as the play progresses, but the only real evidence for this is the suggestion that he has mended the leak in the roof. Against this idea is the fact that he is never seen to get anything else done in the play, and comments by Mick that strongly suggest a complete lack of faith in Aston's ability. Quite early on, Aston says that he will have to put a shade on the light by Davies's bed; again, this is never done. Aston's mental confusion seems to hold him in captivity; it puts a barrier between his ideas and his ability to carry them out, and drains him of the will-power and energy which are necessary for him if he is to get things done.

Aston seems to trust Davies, leaving him alone in the room when he goes out. Perhaps in the offer of the job of caretaker there is a hidden plea for Davies to take care of Aston as well as the house. If so, it is cruelly rejected by the grasping and scheming Davies. Nevertheless, it is possible to feel some sympathy for Davies over his feelings towards Aston. Anyone who has been woken by someone sleep-walking will testify to the terror caused by finding a silent figure gazing down at one's bed. Aston does not sleep-walk, but he does gaze, and his silent smile adds a touch more menace to the picture. He has been in a mental hospital, and most people's fear of the mentally ill would give rise to at least a degree of worry if faced by an ex-patient. However, Aston does seem to be firmly on Davies's side. Mick lets Davies pick up his trousers when Aston enters; and it is Aston who tries to give the bag to Davies when it is brought to the room, even though it is Mick who finally hands it over.

By Act 2 Aston is clearly feeling disturbed by the noise Davies makes in his sleep, but this does not stop him from telling Davies about his experiences in hospital. It is from this speech that the audience learn most about Aston, though Pinter has suggested that it would be wrong to assume that everything Aston says is true. As Pinter does not tell his readers what they should assume, they may wish to classify this comment by Pinter amongst those it is more helpful to forget than to remember. The speech itself has been criticised for sensationalism, and for making capital out of people's fear of mental hospitals and mental illness. But this criticism denies the fact that whatever the morality of the speech, it is very effective on stage purely because of its more sensational aspects. A more valid criticism is that the speech promises much, but achieves relatively little. It is a graphic but quite straightforward description of horrific experiences undergone by a young man. It is difficult to see that it is very much more. It lacks the multi-layered richness so strongly in evidence in Pinter's best writing, and the ability to stimulate the minds of the audience with a wide range of topics and areas.

Aston's room is in a mess. It has already been suggested that the room suggests the confused and disorganised state of Aston's mind, but it is possible to take this one stage further, and say that Aston's attempts to get the room into some sort of order represent humanity's efforts to organise the world in which it lives, attempts which are similarly doomed to failure. This is quite a good and stimulating idea, but taken to extremes it can become extremely silly, as when it is suggested that the 'weight' of the gas cooker which cannot be moved is meant to represent the 'weight' of problems that will have to be solved before the world can be put right. A child's story might have such simplistic correspondence between its symbols and its meaning, but whatever else *The Caretaker* might be, it is neither a children's story, nor simple.

The significance of the shed to Aston, in terms of being a dream and an illusion necessary if he is to survive, has been discussed elsewhere, as has the unusually strong and decisive response Davies's attack on it prompts. More difficult to come to terms with is Aston's relationship with his brother. They appear to have some form of understanding between them, which is suggested by the smile they exchange in the last scene; but beyond this very little information is provided by Pinter. An area of more certainty is the rejection of Davies by Aston. The audience have no reason to doubt Aston's good intentions in bringing Davies into the house, nor his essential kindliness (although some critics have tried to dispose of this view), yet at the end Aston is forced to reject him. For once, the point is made clear: generosity and good intentions are not enough; even a well-meaning person must sometimes deny these impulses when faced with the intransigence of human nature in the shape of Davies. A desire to help others is not enough; those others must have not only the desire to be helped, but also the capacity, and it is the latter that Davies so clearly lacks.

Mick

Of the three characters in *The Caretaker* Mick is the one who says the least, and he is also the one about whom the least can be said. He is in his late twenties, and wears a leather jacket. Some critics have seen this jacket as suggesting the Fascists who pestered Pinter in his youth; but it is probable that the jacket stands for something much wider than this, as in recent times leather jackets, in Western Europe at least, have become associated with violent and rebellious youth.

The audience can never be sure of Mick's motives, or the part he played in Aston's psychiatric treatment. He is a figure of both menace and uncertainty, and both these features owe a great deal to his ability to mix silence and violence. He does no explaining when he assaults Davies at the end of Act 1, and the whole episode is conducted in a frightening silence, until Mick breaks it with the question 'What's the game?' Further confusion is caused by Mick's ability to switch moods suddenly and without warning. After his attack on Davies at the end of Act 1, he suddenly says 'It's awfully nice to meet you'; and he follows the terrifying incident with the vacuum cleaner with the pleasant and innocuous comment 'I was just doing some spring cleaning.' An edge of menace appears in his voice when Davies hints at hostility towards Aston, and at one moment he can be saying to Davies 'I'm very impressed by what you've just said', when only a short while earlier he had been calling him an 'old skate'. Mick seems to delight in confusing Davies with long speeches about who Davies reminds him of, places in London, and professional terminology, all of which serve to confuse Davies's already tottering sense of identity. He taunts Davies with the trousers, the vacuum cleaner, and the bag, and seems also to be trying to trap him into criticising Aston. Mick is also sensitive about his mother, though it is not clear if this is a genuine response, or merely one put on to unsettle Davies further.

Mick seems to be a moderately successful businessman. Aston says he is in the 'building trade', and he certainly seems to know the language of house purchase and interior decorating. He says relatively little to his brother, but there does seem to be some form of understanding between them, even though at one stage he appears exasperated with Aston and ready to deny responsibility for him. Davies describes Mick as 'a bit of a joker', an understatement, for his jokes verge on the macabre. Mick's van was shown in the film of *The Caretaker* so it seems likely that it does exist, and is not just a possible truth thrown out by Pinter.

Mick's major speech comes in Act 3 when he says 'I could turn this place into a penthouse.' This is Mick's dream, and it has already been suggested that this dream could be viewed as 'plastic', hollow, and without substance. Unlike Aston, Mick does not need to be operated on; his dream poses no threat to society, will not shake the world, and can be indulged in without interference from outside sources.

In this speech too a sense of resentment and impatience with Aston can be discerned:

> All this junk here, it's no good to anyone. It's just a load of old iron, that's all. Clobber. You couldn't make a home out of this. There's no way you could arrange it. It's junk. He could never sell it, either, he wouldn't get tuppence for it.

Whatever else Mick is, he is not 'straightforward' as Davies says. In fact the best description of Mick comes from himself, when he is talking about Davies:

> I can take nothing you say at face value. Every word you speak is open to any number of different interpretations. Most of what you say is lies. You're violent, you're erratic, you're just completely unpredictable.

Mick seems possessed by a desire to be on the move, and to impress others with his worldliness:

> Anyone would think this house was all I got to worry about. I got plenty of other things I can worry about. I've got other things. I've got plenty of other interests. I've got my own business to build up, haven't I? I got to think about expanding . . . in all directions. I don't stand still. I'm moving about, all the time, I'm moving . . . all the time. I've got to think about the future.

The staccato repetitions in this speech suggest an almost frantic desire on Mick's part to convince himself, not Davies, that he is in fact 'moving', and that he is a successful businessman. There is a hint of satire in the suggestion that success can only be measured by the number of things a person has to worry about, and his statement that 'I've got to think about the future' can be seen as meaning that he does this in order to stop thinking about the present. Perhaps Mick's attack on Davies parallels Davies's attack on coloured people: when attacking others, they are not thinking about their own deficiencies and failures.

It has been suggested that Mick and Aston represent the two sides of one character, Mick being the actor and Aston the poet. Nearly all interpretations of Pinter's plays are possible; some are not very probable.

The three characters

Pinter has said of *The Caretaker*: 'I do see this play as merely a particular human situation, concerning three particular people, and not, incidentally, symbols.' This suggests that Pinter wants his audiences to see the three characters simply as people, representative of nothing except themselves. Seen in this light, the play is simply a character study, and a study of the way three people react to each other. Certainly the characters in *The Caretaker* are less obviously symbolic than those in Pinter's earlier plays; but even in those plays the audience are usually left in great doubt as to what the characters actually symbolise— so the difference is perhaps more marginal than might at first appear.

The audience also knows more about the characters in *The Caretaker* than they do about those in a play such as *The Birthday Party*. Little explanation is needed as to why Davies, Aston and Mick are as they are in the play, because their portraits are closer to real life than those of characters in other plays, and less an exaggeration of extreme features. Pinter seems to withhold information in his earlier plays deliberately in order to confuse the audience about the antecedents and background of his characters; and whilst the audience do not know a great deal about Davies, Aston and Mick before the play, there is less need to know. The characters explain themselves.

As always with Pinter, the main method of characterisation is through speech. Each character has a distinctive style and tone that is completely his own. That of Davies is grammatically incorrect, full of double negatives, slang, and colloquial shortening of words; and he alternates between whining and aggrieved blustering. Aston's is clipped, monosyllabic, and quietly dignified; while Mick's is bantering, outgoing, and full of jargon, with a hostile energy in much of it.

Plot and technique

The setting for *The Caretaker* is realistic. There is nothing strange about the room, and the house itself is almost certainly thought of by Pinter as being in Hackney, London. This is where the film was set, and Pinter has expressed his delight in the fact that the medium of film allowed the surroundings of the house to be shown. Indeed, everything Pinter has said on this subject suggests that he wished his audiences to be aware that *The Caretaker* was set in a real house in a real setting. If the setting is realistic then the narrative technique (the way Pinter tells his story) is straightforward. He uses no 'flashback' techniques, and allows the play to develop in a chronological sequence of events. This aspect of the play at least is simple, straightforward, and conventional.

Pinter does not preach at his audiences. He does not seem to be putting his own philosophy into the mouth of one of his characters, as many authors have done; and indeed it is doubtful whether he has a philosophy as such to convey. Pinter stands outside his characters, objective and detached, and as a result they are independent creatures with lives of their own, not just aspects of the author's own personality split up into three different facets and given slightly different voices and mannerisms. Pinter has said that his characters 'grow on the page' and 'possess a momentum of their own'. They are created and controlled by the author, but are also allowed to develop in a manner that is consistent with their own reality, and not necessarily in line with the author's first concept of them.

Structure

Each act of *The Caretaker* builds up to a climax at its conclusion: Act 1 with Mick's assault on Davies, Act 2 with Aston's long speech, and Act 3 with Davies's final rejection. It may be purely coincidence that each climax concentrates attention on a different character. The play's unity is strengthened by the insertion of certain incidents or ideas that recur throughout, for example, the draught on Davies's bed, Davies's body odour, the shed, the journey to Sidcup, repetition in different contexts of the words 'stink' and 'skate', and the use of the word 'animal'. Aston's meddling with the same plug is also a recurrent feature.

The basic narrative pattern of the play is clear. Act 1 introduces Davies and Aston, and sees them settle into a semi-stable relationship. Each act is dominated by one of the characters. In Act 1, it is Davies, because it is here that the audience learn most about him and his background. Act 2 introduces Mick, although the audience have seen him before, without hearing him speak or finding out who he is. The entry of Mick may be delayed until Act 2 for dramatic reasons. There are only three characters in the play, and no changes of scene, and by introducing his third character in Act 2 Pinter avoids what otherwise might have been a rather tedious lack of variety in the play. The entry of a new character can usually be guaranteed to stimulate an audience. The second act is dominated by Aston and his concluding speech. Act 3 shows Davies and Mick in what seems to be a friendly mood, and suggests an alliance between them against Aston. The break with Aston does come about as far as Davies is concerned, but at the crucial moment Mick fails to produce the support Davies has been hoping for, and the end of the play returns the audience to the state of affairs that existed at the beginning—Davies the outsider divided by a wide gulf from the other people in the house.

The structure of the play is therefore circular, and the characters in the play are part of this structure, in that despite much talking and arguing they find themselves at the end in exactly the same position as they were at the start. It is as if the characters, like the plot, are locked in a circle out of which they cannot break, and from which the only escape is a dream, be it Sidcup, a shed, or a refurbished house.

Reality and effects

Pinter has admitted that he felt less need in *The Caretaker* to use 'cabaret turns and blackouts and screams in the dark' than he did in his earlier plays. Shock effects and gimmicks are much less in evidence (although light is used with great sensitivity, particularly with regard to the deepening gloom around Aston in his speech about the mental hospital). The example of this that is most often quoted is the difference between the blackouts in *The Birthday Party* and *The Caretaker*. In the former it is explained, without any great conviction or credibility, by the fact that the electricity meter has run out of money; whilst the explanation in *The Caretaker* is visibly true. Mick has taken the light bulb out, for the entirely credible reason that it is the only source of power available for the vacuum cleaner. However it could be argued that the difference between these two incidents is not as great as some critics have suggested. Both are terrifying, both shock the audience, and both evoke a feeling of menace from ordinary domestic events. But on closer examination Mick's explanation does not ring true. In a room full of 'junk' and 'clobber' would he be able to see clearly enough with only the inadequate light on the cleaner itself?

Language and style

Comedy

Explaining a joke is often the quickest way of killing it, but no student can afford to ignore the fact that *The Caretaker* can be a very funny play. This comic element needs to be kept in perspective, as Pinter himself has pointed out, saying that it should not be seen merely as a farce, and that there are 'other issues' at stake in it.

The humour in the play takes many forms. Davies's attempts to present himself as other than he is, as when he says 'I'm clean' or claims to have been propositioned by a woman, are funny because they are so clearly untrue. The audience laugh because they can perceive the weakness that lies beneath the bluster, but it is laughter tinged with sadness, and with equal degrees of sympathy and cruelty. Pinter is an expert in the creation of humour that hinges on a sudden anti-climax, such as when Davies rejects Aston's offered shoes. After praising them at great length he reserves till the end the final and most important fact, that they do not actually fit him. Then there is a rather more absurd type of humour, when a phrase or speech seems totally out of place and takes the audience by surprise with its inconsequentiality. There are numerous examples of this, amongst them Aston's sudden reference to a woman offering to show him her body, Mick's suggestion that Davies might want to buy the house, and his sudden change of tone after terrifying Davies with the vacuum cleaner. The sheer absurdity of a monk saying 'Piss off' is perhaps the classic example of this type of humour. Another type of humour in the play is ironic, when the audience perceive a very different meaning in a word or phrase from that understood by its recipient. An example of this is Mick's remark to Davies about Aston being idle and afraid of work. The audience see in this a direct reference to Davies, as well as to Aston.

Comedy of menace

The phrase 'comedy of menace' is often applied to Pinter's early plays and suggests that although they are funny they are also menacing in a vague and undefined way, unsettling the audience even as they laugh. Pinter has commented in an interview that '. . . more often than not the speech only *seems* to be funny—the man in question is actually fighting a battle for his life.' This element is certainly present in a number of the examples of comedy cited above. Davies being chased by the vacuum cleaner is funny, but for him it is a terrifying experience. Davies's attempts to pretend to be what he is not are funny, but are also a desperate attempt on his part to convince himself as well as others that he is a person worth taking seriously.

The atmosphere of menace is also created by Pinter's ability to drop suddenly from a high comic level to one of deep seriousness, as in Aston's long speech, or Davies's pleading at the end of the play. By this technique the audience are made aware that the comedy is only a surface layer. The sudden outbreaks of violence in the play confirm this and leave the audience unsure of what will come next.

There is fear in the play, fear of Blacks and the men who will come for Davies, fear of the mental hospital, and fear of the unpredictable and violent Mick. Just as Davies is the main vehicle for comedy in the play, so is he the main vehicle for the presentation of fear. He is frightened of the society which he cannot understand and to which he does not belong, frightened at the prospect of being alone again, and frightened of facing up to the truth about himself. Perhaps this fear can also be seen in Mick, with his almost frantic desire to look to the future and keep on the move. The only character who is not frightened of himself is Aston, and his brain has been tampered with. The difference between *The Caretaker* and earlier Pinter plays is that the sources of menace and fear are more readily indentifiable in it; in the earlier plays they tend to be nameless and faceless.

Pinter's language

A London theatre-goer in the early 1950s would generally have gone to plays in which the characters listened to each other, and talked with a degree of intelligence and fluency, without very much offensive language, or slang. This is very different from what is heard in a Pinter play, so different that the term 'Pinteresque' has been evolved by critics as a description of Pinter's language. The term is unpopular with Pinter, and is becoming unpopular with critics simply because it has been used so much that it has lost much of its original meaning. Nevertheless, Pinter's language is distinctive. It has been said that he puts colloquial language under a microscope, showing it as it really is: inconsequential, illogical, repetitious, unwittingly comic, and irrational. Many of these features are to be found in what Davies says. Whatever else Pinter's language may be, it is accurate, catching almost exactly the rhythms and vocabulary of colloquial language. Pauses and silences are frequent stage directions, as they are frequent features of real conversation, and each has a different implication: a pause usually denoting an intense thought process in the mind of the character, a silence signifying a change from one topic to another. However, normal conversation in Pinter's plays can contain moments of great beauty and fluency, and real communication, as well as repetition, slang, and pauses; and some students might consider that Pinter's supposedly real language is simply different language, the opposite side of the coin from that which is usually presented by traditional dramatists.

Character and *The Caretaker*

The Caretaker is one of Pinter's most popular and widely acclaimed plays, but in many ways it is a bridge between two styles. It lacks some of the more absurd elements of *The Room* or *The Birthday Party*, but is not as committed to the examination of personal relationships as, say, *The Homecoming* or *No Man's Land*. An earlier version of the play might well have ended with Davies being murdered, or with all three characters confronting a ruthless and hostile outsider destroying the room; whilst a later version might not have felt the need to have Aston undergo a brain operation, and might have concentrated exclusively on the inter-relationships of the characters. As it stands, the triumph of *The Caretaker* is in its characterisation. Accurate, well-observed, moving, frightening and funny, the characters in *The Caretaker* are its main concern—not what they mean, or even what they do, but simply what they are.

Part 4

Hints for study

Points to select for detailed study

Certain sections of *The Caretaker* are worthy of closer study than that afforded the rest of the play. Davies's speech in Act 1, scene 1 (page 14) where he describes his visit to a monastery gives a good insight into his character and into Pinter's comic techniques. The last three pages of this scene are also vital to a good understanding of the play, as they detail Davies's idea of Sidcup and his papers. The final sequence of Act 1 where Davies is wandering round the room and is attacked by Mick shows him at his most appealing, and is also a good illustration of the violence and menace that are present in the play.

Mick's two speeches in Act 2, scene 1 (pages 31 and 32) are worthy of close study, as they contain much information on Mick's character, the reality of the play, and the theme of menace. Similarly Mick's speech on pages 35–6 ('You're stinking the place out . . .') shows how Mick loves the jargon of modern living, and Davies's fear of this unknown world of papers, agreements, 'down payments', and banks. The incident with the bag reveals the tensions and conflicts at work within the characters. It could be described as 'Pinteresque', as could the opening of Act 2, scene 5 (page 44), where the chasing of Davies by Mick and the vacuum cleaner shows Pinter's ability to create theatrically shocking and effective incidents out of the most common materials. Aston's speech at the end of this act dominates it, and should be studied in depth.

Mick's speech in Act 3, scene 1 (page 60) is vital to an understanding of his particular dream, and the whole of this scene is significant in that it shows Davies attempting to form an alliance with Mick against Aston. The theme of lack of communication is clearly dealt with in Davies's speech at the end of scene 8 ('I've been offered a good job . . .'), and the speech which follows in scene 9 ('What do you expect me to do?') marks the final break between Davies and Aston, reveals his primitive instinct for cruelty and domination, and shows him at his most unattractive. Mick's speeches in scene 10 (pages 73 and 74) are highly revealing about him, and the fact that he has his own tensions and problems to cope with. Davies's speech in Act 3, scene 11 ('You didn't mean that, did you . . .?') is one of the most poignant in the play, and is a comment in depth on the theme of loneliness.

The list of questions at the end of this section shows the type of gen-

eral question that is most frequently asked on the play, and the topics
that examiners usually find most relevant.

Quotations

An effective examination answer must contain quotations. They are the
student's main source of evidence, and without them he or she will be
unable to prove the points made in their answers. Forty lines is a mini-
mum amount to have ready for an examination. The student should
compile his own list of lines to be learnt by writing out on a sheet of
paper all the lines quoted so far and all those given below, and by
selecting a number of lines that will be useful for as wide a range of
answers as possible. Remember to quote exactly, even the punctuation:
falsification of evidence in terms of mis-quotation is seen by examiners
(and rightly so) as a major crime.

Act 1

> I took the lid off a saucepan, you know what was in it? A pile of her
> underclothing, unwashed. The pan for vegetables, it was. The
> vegetable pan.

This is a good example of Pinter's humour.

> Look here, I said to him, I got my rights.

This is a favourite fallacy of Davies. In fact, society allows him no
rights.

> If only the weather would break! Then I'd be able to get down to
> Sidcup!... I got my papers there!

A neat summary of Davies's main concern in life.

> DAVIES: I don't dream. I never dreamed.
> ASTON: No, nor have I.

Ironic lines in the light of their respective dreams of Sidcup and building
the shed.

Act 2

> I could charge seven quid a week for this if I wanted to.

Mick seems to need to believe that his house is valuable.

> No, what I need, is a kind of shirt with stripes, a good solid shirt,
> with stripes going down.

These lines show Pinter's comic technique, and the pathetic choosiness of Davies.

> Well, I mean, you don't know who might come up them front steps, do you? I got to be a bit careful.

This shows Davies's fear of the outside world, and the theme of menace.

> But she signed their form, you see, giving them permission. I know that because he showed me her signature when I brought it up.

An illustration of the theme of betrayal.

> But I want to do something first. I want to build that shed out in the garden.

Aston's dream neatly summarised.

Act 3

> MICK: Well you say you're an interior decorator, you'd better be a good one.

These lines mark the turning point for Davies, and put the seal on his eviction from the house.

> DAVIES: I didn't tell you nothing! Won't you listen to what I'm saying?

An excellent summary of the theme of lack of communication, and also an illustration of Davies's use of double negatives.

> DAVIES: But you don't understand my meaning!

Another illustration of lack of communication.

Effective arrangement of material

There are a number of basic rules which apply to the writing of any examination answer. The first is relevance. The student who simply writes down everything he knows about a book or play, regardless of the question he has been asked, will fail, just as surely as the student who knows nothing at all. Planning is equally important when the student is working to a strict time limit. It is also vital to come to a firm conclusion in answers, and not to leave the issue contained in the question undecided. Finally, the student should present all sides of an argument, and not just those points that support his own particular view. An essay that presents the facts for only one side of an argument is in-effective. However strongly a particular viewpoint may be held and argued, the reader can only accept that viewpoint completely if he is shown why the other possible interpretations are not correct.

Planning an answer

There are four stages in the writing of an effective plan, and these need take no longer than five or six minutes in an examination. A typical question on *The Caretaker* might be: 'To what extent should *The Caretaker* be interpreted as a play of social criticism?' This question has been chosen for an example of planning technique because an answer to it can be divided up fairly simply into a number of readily definable categories, making it easier to perceive the structure of the planning technique. However, the technique readily adapts to questions that are rather more vague.

(a) Note down rough ideas

When the student first sees a question, ideas for an answer will come into his head immediately. These should be put down in note form, with no attempt as yet to organise them into paragraphs:

Society is criticised in that it does not care for either Davies or Aston. It does not treat its casualties. Perhaps in Aston it creates them.
Does Davies deserve to be cared for?
Society attacks and destroys artists and dissidents.
Racial prejudice.
Paperwork and paraphernalia of modern living criticised, British worker criticised, false values criticised.
No character readily identifiable as agent of society.
Is what Aston says true? Was he a dangerous maniac before his operation?
Are characters just individuals, seen apart from society?
Very little of society seen in play—just three people and a room.
Other (more important?) themes: communication
                                       loneliness
                                       dreams and illusion
                                       identity
Is it life that is shown as being miserable, regardless of society?
Is the state and predicament of Davies society's fault, or his own?

A student who walks into an examination and starts writing immediately will produce what can be seen above, namely an essay that is fragmented, disorganised, and repetitive. The basic materials from which a convincing answer can be built are there, but have just been dumped in random order on the site. The next stage is to put them in the right sequence.

(b) Paragraph rough ideas

The next stage is to group the rough preliminary ideas into paragraphs. Perhaps new ideas will occur to the writer, in which case they should be added to the plan at what seems to be the best point. The main aim is to delete ideas that occur more than once, and put ideas of a similar nature together in paragraphs.

1. *Criticisms of society*
   Not treating its casualties, and creating them
   Society destroys artists and dissidents
   Criticisms of racial prejudice
           paperwork
           British worker
           false values

2. *Weaknesses*
   Perhaps Davies does not deserve to be cared for; he has brought his state on by his own actions
   Aston could be lying, could have been dangerous
   Racial prejudice and British worker criticisms based on one character (Davies); need he represent society in general?
   Play centred on only three characters and one room; how representative of society can all this be?

3. *Other interpretations*
   Criticisms of society only small part of what is said. More significant themes are communication
           loneliness
           dreams and illusion
           identity
           menace

In grouping the ideas a number of changes have taken place. This is normal and even desirable, and shows that the student's mind is already working on the information and shaping it as he thinks more about the question. This is a major advantage of planning an essay: it gives the student more time to think about what he is writing, and to understand the question fully.

(c) Put paragraphs in order and write conclusion

Only at this stage can the student decide what his answer to the question will be, because only now does he have all the information in front of him. It is very common for an examination candidate to rush into the examination room, make an instant decision on the answer to the question before him, and then find half-way through writing that he actually has more evidence in favour of the view he thought he was opposing. The conclusion should depend on the evidence; if there is more of it to suggest that *The Caretaker* is not primarily a play of social criticism, then that must be the answer, regardless of what the student previously thought. It is also useful to argue throughout the essay, and not just give one's view in a conclusion. Conclusions are often a cause of great concern and worry to students, and a common idea is that the student has to find some startling new piece of evidence in them, something to end the essay in a blaze of glory, which will impress the examiner with the student's skill and breadth of knowledge. This is a fallacy. A conclusion should contain a brief survey of all the points made in the essay so that the examiner is left at the end with a clear idea of what has been said. No new ideas should be included in the conclusion. If the ideas are worthwhile there will be no time at the end of the essay to deal with them in sufficient depth, and if they are not worthwhile they should not be in the essay at all. What is useful sometimes is a quotation from the text, the author, or even a critic, which sums up the viewpoint expressed in the essay, or backs up one of its main points.

The order in which paragraphs occur is of vital significance, and the student should group them as far as possible in a logical sequence where the ideas follow on from what has been said before. In the case of the specimen plan, the paragraphs already follow such an order, with the points *for* the play being social criticism first, and those *against* this idea last. This is the best order. The student should always put the arguments for the view he does *not* support first in his essay, so as to make a strong statement at the end.

(d) Write topic sentences/find evidence

Before actually writing the answer, each paragraph must be given a topic sentence. This is the first sentence in a paragraph, and it states in a few words what the subject or point of that paragraph is. It is useful because it gives the reader an immediate grasp of what is being said, and because it allows the writer to check quickly and easily whether what he is saying is relevant to the question. If the topic sentence is not a direct answer to the question, or firmly on the lines laid down by it, then the paragraph which follows is not relevant, and should be deleted. The topic sentence also cures another fault, that of producing a long string of evidence and facts with only a few weak sentences at the end of the paragraph to say what the student thinks this evidence proves. This forces the examiner to read through a great weight of material without knowing what its point is, and hence without knowing whether it is good use of evidence or bad. By the time the point is made at the end of the paragraph the examiner will have forgotten much of the evidence, and may not take the trouble to go back and check whether it was relevant or not. The topic sentence tells the examiner the point the student is trying to make, and after it he can judge effectively the evidence that is produced in favour of this point.

The final stage of planning is to assemble quotations and evidence to prove whatever is being said.

Below are four specimen answers, the first being the one that might have been written from the above plan. Bear in mind that these are only possible answers, and not necessarily the only ones that are right.

To what extent should *The Caretaker* be interpreted as a play of social criticism?

The dramatists who came to prominence in Britain in the mid-1950s, such as John Osborne and Arnold Wesker, were often very concerned with the workings and nature of society in their plays, and frequently hostile, or at least critical of it. The same cannot be said of Pinter, although it is possible to see quite a large amount of social criticism in *The Caretaker*.

A number of aspects of society appear to come under criticism in the play. In their different ways both Davies and Aston are casualties of society, Davies because he cannot cope with its complexity and Aston because he has a damaged mentality, and no attempt is made by society to integrate them. Davies seems doomed to perpetual loneliness and isolation, a person existing only on the very fringe of society, whilst Aston, also lonely, relies on the unpredictable companionship of his brother. Both characters are unfulfilled. It could also be argued that society has made Davies and Aston what they are, Aston by operating on him and Davies by never giving him trust and being hostile towards him. As Davies says:

> You been a good friend to me. You took me in. You took me in, you didn't ask me no questions, you give me a bed . . .

It would appear from his tone that no one else has done these small services for Davies. Aston can be seen as a symbol of the artist or dissident, the talker whose talk does not always agree with what the forces of society would have him say: 'I talked too much. That was my mistake.' As such Aston posed a threat to society, which responded with a terrifying operation that clamped down his personality, and reduced him to conformity at the expense of his personality and individuality.

Racial prejudice is also criticised in the play, with Davies using his hatred of coloured people to boost his own sense of superiority and excuse his own faults, as when he blames the noise he makes in the night on the 'Blacks' in the other rooms. The paraphernalia and paperwork of modern living is attacked and made fun of, as when Mick refers to 'twenty per cent interest, fifty per cent deposit; down payments, back payments, family allowances, bonus schemes, remission of term for good behaviour, six months lease, yearly examination of the relevant archives . . .' and so on, in what can seem an endless list. The dreams of modern society are also criticised, where all a man can yearn for is 'Deep azure-blue carpet, unglazed blue and white curtains, a bedspread with a pattern of small blue roses on a white ground . . .', and where one must always look to the future, not to the present. Davies, with his insistence on his 'rights', his laziness, and his acquisitiveness, can be seen as a symbol of the British worker, also under fire in the play.

However, these arguments for the play being a piece of social criticism are not as convincing as they might at first appear. Society rejects Davies; but it may be that he deserves to be rejected. He is a filthy, whining, aggressive personality, not much removed from the 'wild animal' that Mick calls him. He viciously attacks the one person who has helped him, tries to destroy the harmony of the house which has taken him in, ignores his own shortcomings, and is totally lacking in generosity. In theory society might be expected to offer him a helping hand; in practice it seems justified in not so doing, if his behaviour with Aston is typical of what he does to those who try to help him.

Pinter has suggested that the audience need not believe everything Aston says. The description that he gives of himself as he was before the operation is vague enough for him to have been an artistic personality or a dissident, but also vague enough for him to have been dangerously insane. If this is the case then society could be right in trying to render him harmless. Racial prejudice and criticism of the British worker are both lodged in one person, Davies, and it may well be just one individual who is being criticised, or a type of person, not society as a whole. Indeed, in a play which contains only three characters and one room there appears to be an insufficiently wide base on which to rest a criticism of society at large. It is much more a study of three separate, individual people, and the way they relate to each other. Pinter has said:

> When a character cannot be comfortably defined or understood in terms of the familiar, the tendency is to perch him on a symbolic shelf, out of harm's way.

Those who see the play as a piece of social criticism are seeking to make symbols out of the characters, instead of recognising them as individuals.

To interpret *The Caretaker* as social criticism is to ignore the greater part of what it sets out to do. It has an element of social criticism in it, but this is overshadowed by its other thematic concerns, such as communication, loneliness, dreams and illusion, identity, and menace. There is no figure representing society in the play, but there are three who show humanity's desperate need to communicate and its tragic inability either to make that communication or accept it when it is offered. They are characters who manage to exist in their world only by fixing their eyes on some aim or hope in the future (Sidcup, Aston's shed, Mick's redecorated room), so that present misery and hopelessness can be ignored, or at least temporarily overlooked.

Pinter has said '. . . I'm not conscious of any particular social function'; and he is a writer who refuses to be pinned down to easy social criticisms. Society is criticised in *The Caretaker*, but only in passing and without any great conviction. *The Caretaker* is a play about individuals, not society as a whole.

How realistic is *The Caretaker*?

Realism is a notoriously difficult word to define. In the sense of being closest to real life, the ultimate realistic book would spend eight hours with its characters whilst they slept, take every mouthful of food with them, and describe every time they went to the toilet. There are books which come close to doing this—such as James Joyce's *Ulysses* (1922)—but not completely, and nearly all works of literature are unrealistic at least in the sense that they present selections from life and exaggerations of it, rather than showing the reader the whole thing.

There are certainly a number of incidents in *The Caretaker* which can be seen as unrealistic. It does not seem likely that in modern Britain Aston would be sent to a mental hospital simply because he talked too much, or that an operation would involve a conscious patient having pincers put on his head and being treated in such a horrific manner. Nor is it likely that a monk would tell a man to 'Piss off'. Mick often speaks and behaves in an unrealistic manner. It is certainly not normal for a person to chase someone else in a darkened room with a vacuum cleaner; or for him suddenly to turn on someone and insist (falsely) that he had said he was a qualified interior decorator. Much of what Mick says can appear unrealistic:

> Long-jump specialist. He had a habit of demonstrating different run-ups in the drawing room round about Christmas time. He had a penchant for nuts. That's what it was. Nothing else but a penchant. Couldn't eat enough of them . . . Had a marvellous stop watch. Picked it up in Hong Kong. The day after they chucked him out of the Salvation Army. Used to go in number four for Beckenham reserves.

The audience might well have trouble believing in the existence of this athletic, ex-Salvation Army, well-travelled, football-playing nut addict.

It is necessary to distinguish between what is unrealistic, and what is simply unusual, abnormal, or uncertain. It is unusual and abnormal for a person to commit murder, in the sense that only a tiny percentage of the whole population does so, but it is a perfectly realistic thing to happen: it happens, and is known to happen, all the time. Aston's operation is abnormal and unusual, but it could have happened. The monk's saying 'Piss off' becomes realistic if it is seen as Davies translating what was said into his own language, and not as a literal account of what was actually said. Mick's speeches and his chasing of Davies with a vacuum cleaner can also be made to appear realistic: the speeches once one realises that they are a conscious attempt to confuse and unsettle Davies, the vacuum cleaner episode by the explanation that Mick himself provides.

There are a large number of very realistic and true-to-life elements in the play to set against the relatively few unreal ones. *The Caretaker* is set, as the film made clear, in Hackney, London, and throughout real names are used for towns and areas (Luton, Shepherd's Bush, Sidcup). There is nothing unrealistic about either the background or the room itself. Thus the audience are continually reminded of the real world that exists outside the room, and with which all three characters have or have had contact. The characters look realistic: they have no visible physical deformities, they suffer from draughts and cannot sleep, and their clothes are perfectly normal for their station in life.

Above all Pinter's language is realistic. It is not the formal, artificial, studied language of classical drama, but a re-creation of the rhythms and style of real speech. It has the pauses and unfinished sentences of colloquial speech:

ASTON: Till you . . . get yourself fixed up.
DAVIES: (*sitting*). Ay well, that . . .
ASTON: Get yourself sorted out . . .
DAVIES: Oh, I'll be fixed up . . . pretty soon now . . .
Pause

It has the repetition and inconsequentiality of real speech:

I said to this monk, here, I said, look here, mister, he opened the door, big door, he opened it, look here, mister, I said, I come all the way down here, look, I said, I showed him these, I said, you haven't got a pair of shoes, have you, a pair of shoes, I said . . .

The order of ideas in this speech is not logical, nor is the grammar correct ('come' should be 'came' or 'have come'), but it is an accurate reflection of the way a character such as Davies might speak. Pinter's language is full of slang and colloquial terms, such as 'arse', 'skate', 'flog it', 'bastard', 'en't' (for 'isn't it?') and so on.

The particular realism of *The Caretaker* goes deeper than external features such as clothing and physical setting. It is psychological reality. The main themes displayed through the characters—loneliness, failure of communication, generosity, selfishness, a desire to protect one's own territory—are basic features of human nature, to be found in any age and at any time. Davies, in particular, manifests characteristics that must be all too familiar to any adult human. His pathetic desire for companionship coupled with his inability to sustain it represents all those people whose desire for happiness is continually thwarted by weakness of character. Everyone knows the reality of loneliness, of not being able to say what one feels, of rejection; and there is no feature in the play more real than Davies's desperation when he says 'What am I going to do?' Only with Aston do the standards of reality slip a little in the play. He is an enigmatic, reduced figure, not a complete individual, and the degree of artificiality in his character makes him the least realistic person in the play.

There are unreal elements in *The Caretaker*, for the most part centred on Aston, but these are outweighed by the many other elements which link the play firmly to the real world. In setting, in language, and in the appearances and problems of its characters, *The Caretaker* is triumphantly real.

What part does comedy play in *The Caretaker*, and how does Pinter achieve his comic effects?

Pinter's early plays are often described as 'comedies of menace', and Pinter himself has admitted that the audience are meant to laugh in the play. He has also said that the play is not simply a farce, and that there is more to it than just comedy.

Pinter uses a variety of techniques to gain his comic effects. One of these is incongruity, where a speech or episode is so unexpected, so out of place, that it becomes funny. Davies's suggestion that a monk told him to 'Piss off' is an example of this; as is Mick's sudden and playful assumption that Davies is in a position to buy his house:

> No argument. I mean, if that sort of money's in your range don't be afraid to say so. Here you are. Furniture and fittings, I'll take four hundred or the nearest offer.

Much of the comedy in the play is ironical: the audience are able to see that what a character says and what he means are two different things. An example of this is Mick's comment to Davies that Aston is 'work-shy'. He appears to be talking about Aston, but is in fact talking about Davies. Pinter is skilful at creating sudden anti-climaxes which are comic. After a highly enthusiastic description of a pair of shoes that

Aston has offered him, during which the audience are led to believe that he will accept them, Davies announces that they 'Don't fit though'. Another anti-climax occurs when after terrorising and assaulting Davies Mick suddenly says 'It's awfully nice to meet you.' Again, this takes the audience by surprise, and so causes them to laugh.

There is comedy of a more subtle type in the self-deceptions of the characters, such as Davies's idea that he will go to Sidcup, and his protestation to Aston that a woman has invited him to see her body. Davies's 'choosiness' is funny, because a man in his position might be expected to accept gratefully anything that is offered him; so is his ignorance, as when he fears that a gas cooker that is not connected could poison him. The main vehicle for the comedy in the play is Davies, and it has been suggested that he is the comic in the play whilst Aston and Mick are the 'straight men', lacking in humour in order to emphasise that coming from Davies.

However, there is more than laughter in a number of the comic episodes. The audience's laughter can act like a knife that cuts through the layers of deception which the characters try to erect around themselves, so that while they are laughing the audience are revealing the true nature of the character being laughed at. There is also quite often a hint of menace in the laughter. Mick's chasing of Davies with a vacuum cleaner is funny, but also terrifying, and whilst Davies's racial prejudice is comic because it is so clearly based on ignorance and insensitivity, the laughter it produces may nevertheless leave a slightly bitter taste behind.

Pinter has said that laughter can conceal a battle for survival, and this can be clearly seen in the play. Davies's attempts to justify himself and gain a dominant position in the house are funny because they are so transparent, but for Davies they are not funny: they are a matter of life and death, as his broken pleading in the final act shows. There are moments of high drama in *The Caretaker*, such as Aston's speech and the final scene of the play; and the comedy in the play emphasises and highlights these through the medium of contrast.

The comedy in *The Caretaker* springs from Pinter's ability to place people under a microscope, and show the audience their characters with all their illogicality, irrationality, and weaknesses. It is also like the sugar coating round an unpleasant-tasting pill. It amuses and entertains the audience whilst at the same time making points of immense seriousness and sensitivity. *The Caretaker* is not a comedy, but a mixture of comedy and tragedy, which can change instantly from a richly-comic mood to a near tragic one. Comedy is not a theme of the play, but merely one of the techniques by which Pinter conveys a multi-layered portrait of three characters, and discusses such themes as loneliness, failure of communication, and dream and illusion.

To what extent should Davies be seen as an Everyman figure, and a symbolic representation of humanity?

A number of critics have insisted on seeing the characters in many of Pinter's plays not just as portraits drawn from life but as symbolic or allegorical representations. *The Caretaker* is no exception, and there is one school of thought that suggests Davies should be seen as Everyman, or a figure whose character, problems, and life can be seen as representative of certain basic features that are shared by every human being.

Many of the characteristics that go to make up the portrait of Davies are certainly representative, in the sense that they can be found quite frequently amongst ordinary people. He has no special skills or abilities that mark him out from the common run of humanity. He is not gifted intellectually, or in any other sense, nor is he exceptional at the other end of the scale: although he is old, he has no physical deformity or chronic bad health. From these facts it is possible to deduce that he is an ordinary human being, someone whom the audience could quite readily see as being drawn from real life.

Davies's problems are not unique, and are very much a part of normal human existence. He tries pathetically to cling to his dignity when society and other people are seeking to strip him of it:

> Look here, I said to him, I got my rights. I told him that. I might have been on the road but nobody's got more rights than I have. Let's have a bit of fair play, I said.

He is frightened of loneliness and anything he does not understand, such as the technicalities of taxation, house purchase, and 'papers', as are most humans, although their fears are not normally of things as practical as these. Nevertheless, the inexperienced person might well feel a twinge of sympathy for Davies, especially after having completed a tax form, embarked on house purchase, or been faced with a lengthy and complex questionnaire from a government agency. Davies's fear of 'down payments, back payments, family allowances, bonus schemes' is common enough to make it a standard human reaction. It may be that in Davies Pinter is showing his audiences an even more basic human instinct, that of territorial advantage, or the desire to gain dominance in any given situation. Davies certainly shows this in his dealings with Aston and Mick. His belief that he will 'sort himself out' when he gets down to Sidcup can be seen as representing all the things that people dream of doing, but never achieve. The belief that the next move or the next job will bring fulfilment, that the marriage will improve if only the couple can get a good holiday, that the children would get good examination results if only the teaching they received were a little better, all these are comparable to Davies and his dream of Sidcup. All are desperate vehicles for hope, and attempts to postpone a painful realisation. Davies represents all people who try to evade reality by dreams and fantasies. When he says 'you don't understand my meaning!' he can be seen as representative of all the people who fail to communicate with others. Davies is selfish, proud, and incapable of seeing his own mistakes, all of which, albeit regrettably, are very common features amongst people.

There are other areas in which Davies can be said to represent more than just his own self. His language is that of the common man (or at least the common man brought up in southern England). Like many an Everyman figure, he is a wanderer who meets trials and tribulations on his journeyings. Like a number of religious figures he is poor, unmarried, and is rejected by his fellow men, and in this respect at least he can be compared to Jesus. It has even been said that Aston and Mick represent the forces of good and evil to be found in the world, forces which Davies as Everyman must face and come to terms with. If Davies is Everyman and the allegory is along the lines suggested by this interpretation, then it would appear that Pinter has little hope for humanity, because Davies singularly fails to come to terms with either force.

The above list makes a powerful case for seeing Davies as Everyman, but closer examination suggests that this interpretation must be subject to considerable reservations and qualifications. To see Davies as representative of all humanity is to ignore many of his most obvious features. He is an outcast before he is rescued by Aston, an unprincipled vagrant, and a filthy, ill-clothed wreck of a man. Certainly there are many people like Davies in the world, but he is nevertheless an extreme case, a total loss to society, and hardly typical of all humanity. If he were, society would have ceased to exist thousands of years ago.

Davies's problems are common enough for an audience to feel a degree of sympathy for him, and they are clearly drawn from the real world. Davies shows the dark side of life, in the form of loneliness, rejection, inadequacy, loss of personal identity, and failure, but however compelling the portrait might be, it is only of one side of life. A true Everyman figure, such as Christian in John Bunyan's *Pilgrim's Progress* (1675), has to face the problems of success, of spirituality, of family, as well as those faced by Davies. Davies is a portrait of failure, but failure, however common, is only one aspect of life. Furthermore, to compare a figure such as Davies with Jesus, or any religious leader or prophet, is both laughable and sacrilegious; at least until such time as a religious leader can be found who is or was a liar, totally selfish, filthy, ungrateful, totally lacking in generosity, foul-mouthed, scurrilous, and violent. Davies is all these things, and as a result Davies is not unusual, but equally is not a representative of all humanity.

Pinter has said that his characters should be seen as characters, and not as symbols, and *The Caretaker* would seem to support this idea. Davies is a representative figure, but the vision is limited to one part of the human experience. This makes it no less compelling and vivid, but it does mean that Davies should be seen not as Everyman, but simply as part of man.

Questions

1. Does Pinter mean his audience to sympathise with Davies, or condemn him?
2. Discuss the theme of menace in *The Caretaker*.
3. What are the main features of Pinter's use of language in *The Caretaker*?
4. Is it true to say that Aston is the least convincing and effective character in *The Caretaker*?
5. Explore in detail the relationship between Aston and Mick in *The Caretaker*.
6. What role does violence play in *The Caretaker*?
7. Discuss the theme of the room in *The Caretaker*.
8. 'But you don't understand my meaning!' Discuss the theme of communication in *The Caretaker*.
9. Is it accurate to describe *The Caretaker* as a pessimistic play?
10. 'Three characters running away from themselves.' Discuss this description of *The Caretaker*.
11. 'A theatrical fraud.' How far would you agree that *The Caretaker* 'promises much, but achieves little'?
12. Discuss the role of dream and illusion in *The Caretaker*.
13. How does Pinter maintain the interest of the audience in a play with only three characters, and set throughout in the same room?
14. Comment briefly on Pinter's use of (a) pauses and silences (b) clothing (c) lighting effects.
15. 'Pinter's effects depend on a slight distortion of the everyday in language and character.' Discuss with reference to *The Caretaker*.
16. 'The drama is conveyed not only by what we see and hear, but by what we do not see, do not hear.' How true is this of *The Caretaker*?
17. 'It is often least realistic when it is closest to actuality.' Discuss with reference to *The Caretaker*.
18. 'Pinter's greatest skill lies in making the abnormal appear normal.' Discuss.
19. How true is it to say that the plot and structure of *The Caretaker* are based on 'a see-saw motion, alternating between peace and violence, tension and relaxation'?
20. 'The theme of *The Caretaker* is that no one does take care—least of all of other people.' Discuss.

Part 5

Suggestions for further reading

The text

PINTER, HAROLD: *The Caretaker*. Methuen, London, 1960; revised edition 1962.
The text used for this study is the revised paperback edition published in 1962.

Other works by Harold Pinter

Certain individual play titles are listed below; however, the best buy for the student is probably the three-volume edition listed below which contains all Pinter's work (and some interviews and comments from him on it) up to 1968.
The Birthday Party. Eyre Methuen, London, revised edition 1965.
The Homecoming. Eyre Methuen, London, 1965; revised editions 1966 and 1967.
No Man's Land. Eyre Methuen, London, 1975.
Betrayal. Eyre Methuen, London, 1978.
Plays: One. Eyre Methuen, London, 1976.
Plays: Two. Eyre Methuen, London, 1977.
Plays: Three. Eyre Methuen, London, 1978.

Criticism

BAKER, WILLIAM, and TABACHNICK, STEPHEN: *Harold Pinter*. Oliver & Boyd, Edinburgh, 1973. This book gives a very full and enlightening treatment of the Jewish element in Pinter's work.
ESSLIN, MARTIN: *Pinter: A Study Of His Plays*. Eyre Methuen, London, 1977. Originally published under the title *The Peopled Wound: The Plays of Harold Pinter*, this is the standard reference work on Pinter, and is invaluable.
GANZ, ARTHUR (ED.): *Pinter: A Collection Of Critical Essays*. Prentice-Hall (Spectrum Books), New Jersey, 1972. This contains some interesting essays, but is a book for the advanced student.

HAYMAN, RONALD: *Harold Pinter*. Contemporary Playwrights Series, Heinemann, London, 1975. A rather cursory but very readable survey of all Pinter's plays.

HINCHLIFFE, ARNOLD: *Harold Pinter*. Twayne's English Authors Series, Twayne, New York, 1967. Griffin Authors Series, Macmillan, London, 1976. This work contains a very useful survey of other criticism on Pinter, and is a useful introductory book.

KERR, WALTER: *Harold Pinter*. Columbia Essays on Modern Writers No. 27, Columbia University Press, New York and London, 1967. Another useful survey of Pinter's work.

TAYLOR, JOHN RUSSELL: *Harold Pinter*. Writers and Their Work No. 212, Longman, London, 1969; revised edition 1973. A short pamphlet by one of the leading critics of Pinter's work.

This is only a brief selection from some of the more outstanding books written on Pinter.

Background

ESSLIN, MARTIN: *The Theatre of the Absurd*. Penguin Books, Harmondsworth, revised edition 1968. A very influential book giving useful background information for a study of Pinter.

TAYLOR, JOHN RUSSELL: *Anger and After*. Methuen, London, 1962. One of the best works available on British theatre in the 1950s.

The author of these notes

MARTIN STEPHEN was educated at Uppingham, the University of Leeds, and the University of Sheffield. He is at present a housemaster and teacher of English at Haileybury College. He is the author of five titles in the *York Notes* series. He has made several appearances on radio and television as a folk musician. At present he is working on a book about the poetry of the First World War.